The

# Nelly Butler

# Hauntings

*A Documentary History*

Edited by

## Marcus LiBrizzi and Dennis Boyd

Library of Early Maine Literature
University of Maine at Machias

2010

LIBRARY OF EARLY MAINE LITERATURE

Cover design by Dan Barr. Photograph by Marcus LiBrizzi
Book design by Marcus LiBrizzi and Loni Levesque.

ISBN: 978-0-615-39496-1

Book Orders and Catalogs:

> LIBRARY OF EARLY MAINE LITERATURE
> Kimball Hall
> University of Maine at Machias
> 116 O'Brien Avenue
> Machias, ME USA  04654
>
> earlymainelit@maine.edu
>
> www.machias.edu/earlymainelit

Suggested Cataloging-in-Publication Data:

> LiBrizzi, Marcus A., 1964-
> Boyd, Dennis W., 1950-
> The Nelly Butler Hauntings: A Documentary History/
> Marcus LiBrizzi and Dennis Boyd, editors.
> Includes bibliographical references.
> ISBN:  978-0-615-39496-1
> 1. Ghost stories, American—Maine. 2. Sullivan (Me.)
> 3. Spiritualist Movement, American, History, 18th century.
> 4.  Nelly Butler, 1776-1797.

❋❋❋
# TABLE OF CONTENTS
❋❋❋

❈ ❈ ❈

# THE NELLY BUTLER HAUNTINGS: AN UNSOLVED MYSTERY
## BY MARCUS LIBRIZZI

❈ ❈ ❈

"Pause, reader, and consider a few moments what evidence would convince you of the existence of a specter."[1] Thus states an eye-witness on the most famous haunting in Early America. This is the tale of the Nelly Butler apparition, who appeared to more than one hundred individuals and directed the course of events on the coast of Maine in 1799-1800. Despite the historical and cultural significance of the event, its primary sources have slumbered for almost two hundred years in an obscure and virtually inaccessible book. The present edition makes these sources available, supplementing them through explanatory notes, research, and supporting materials. The result is a documentary history on an unsolved mystery.

For a number of reasons, the Nelly Butler hauntings stand out as remarkable. Robert Ellis Cahill referred to the case as "the first recorded and documented ghost story in American history."[2] The spectacular series of supernatural appearances took place in Sullivan, Maine, little more than fifteen years after the American Revolution. In writing the original account, Abraham Cummings paved the way for the scientific inquiry of paranormal phenomena. He included in his account thirty-seven letters, depositions, and testimonies from people who had witnessed the apparition. "I took these [...] from their lips, for the most part, separately. I wrote them, read them in their hearing, and obtained their approbation of what I had written."[3] These documents, in their colorful vernacular, provide multiple perspectives on the ghostly manifestations and give to the Cummings' text an extremely rare form of documentation in such an early study of the supernatural.

The mass sightings of the Nelly Butler apparition form the true origin of the spiritualist movement in the United States. The conventional starting point is 1848 in the séances conducted by the Fox sisters in Hydesville and Rochester, New York.[4] But as stated by Joseph Citro, the trend "began a good half-century before" in the Nelly Butler apparition, "one of the most witnessed ghosts in history."[5] Crowds of people encountered the phantom on more than thirty occasions. Spiritualism, which concerns the efforts to contact and communicate with spirits, became enormously popular in the 19th century, shaping popular culture and formal history, with séances even conducted at the White House. To the present day, spiritualism is a force to be reckoned with, ascribed to by millions, and this mass movement ironically started in the tiny coastal village of Sullivan, located fifteen miles by water from Bar Harbor, Maine.

On the wooden ships departing from Sullivan Harbor, the tales of the strange specter spread to distant ports. "The talk about the [...] spirit became general in this and the surrounding towns and all over the county," wrote one account, "and people came from long distances to witness its manifestations. Abner Blaisdell was a religious man and his house became famous as a resort for meetings of prayer and singing and hearing the knockings."[6] As stated by Muriel Roll, the Nelly Butler apparition "prepared the ground in this country for the acceptance and spread of spiritualist rappings and allied phenomena in the middle of the nineteenth century."[7] In addition, "several details that are now conventional features of the séance probably made their debut on the American scene in this case."[8] In 1859, spiritualists in Portland, Maine, reissued the history of the Nelly Butler hauntings, documenting a dramatic starting point for their movement.[9]

For many writers, the specter calling itself Nelly Butler was among the most convincing of recorded apparitions. Yet few other hauntings created such a storm of controversy, sparking accusations of fraud, witchcraft, and demonism. The primary setting for the specter that called itself Nelly Butler was the cellar of the Blaisdell house in Sullivan, but the ghost appeared in at least four other dwellings in the community, and it could manifest itself outside, in the day and in the middle of the night. Increasingly large groups of people witnessed the spirit during the main period of its manifestations in August of 1800. The climax of spiritual encounters took place in a funereal march on the night of August 13-14, 1800. At this time, the Nelly Butler apparition followed a procession of nearly fifty people through the village to the house of a vocal disbeliever, James Miller. The specter spoke in his house, then appeared outside in a field before following the people back to the Blaisdell House. While the phantom mainly conversed on religious topics, it also spoke on personal matters, and it orchestrated at least two events: the re-interment of Nelly Butler's child, and the marriage of her former husband, George Butler, to a young woman named Lydia Blaisdell. For some detractors of the spirit, the phantom was also instrumental in the death of this young woman. We'd have to agree with William Oliver Stevens when he wrote that "in sum total it may make a strong claim [...] to being the most extraordinary ghost story on record."[10]

The hauntings commenced in the winter of 1799, inside the Blaisdell House, which once stood on the granite shores of Taunton Bay in Sullivan. A young woman of the house, Lydia Blaisdell, was stricken with pestilence, perhaps contracted during a trip to the Boston area. During the long period of her convalescence back in Maine, the ghost first manifested itself in Lydia's home through mysterious knocking and rapping sounds coming from the cellar. As stated in the earliest account, "the very first notices of anything unaccountable were given at the time when Lydia Blaisdell [...] was at the point of death."[11]   After thorough searches of the cellar failed to turn up anything to account for the strange sounds, "the family prayed together, that, if there was deception in this extraordinary injunction, the Lord would make it known to them, and that, if the cause was of God, they might be preserved."[12]

By December, a disembodied voice began speaking from the Blaisdell cellar.  The spectral voice announced itself as the spirit of a young local woman named Nelly Butler, who died three years earlier.  Nelly Butler's fame came to her as an apparition; little information exists regarding the actual woman.  She appeared in this world as Eleanor Hooper, born on April 25, 1776, in Franklin, Maine, a village located next to Sullivan.[13]   At nineteen, Nelly married George Butler, a young sea captain from a prominent family who lived nearby. Following a disastrous childbirth, Nelly Butler died on June 13th, 1797, probably twenty-four hours after the burial of her baby.[14] According to local lore, Nelly's grave is located on Butler's Point, in Franklin, Maine, next to the remains of her child, her husband, and Tugwassah, a Native American who befriended the settlers.[15]   There are, however, no headstones with inscriptions to confirm the identity of the fieldstone grave markers located out on the peninsula.

The hauntings by the Nelly Butler apparition comprised two phases.  In the first, lasting from December 1799 to May 1800, the specter had a peculiar mission.  The apparition in the Blaisdell cellar declared that it had returned from the grave to orchestrate the marriage of Nelly Butler's widower, George Butler, to Lydia Blaisdell.   Due to the difference in age between the couple, there was great objection to their connection, particularly by Abner Blaisdell, Lydia's father. In 1800, Lydia Blaisdell was only fifteen years old, and George Butler was twenty-nine.[16]  It was customary for women in the region at this time to marry at eighteen or nineteen years of age, yet instances existed of brides as young as fourteen or fifteen.[17]   At any rate, accounts of the courtship between George Butler and Lydia Blaisdell noted a history of opposition. Before the specter convinced Abner Blaisdell otherwise, he maintained a "notorious and inflexible opposition to this connection, which had continued several years."[18]

The ghost's disembodied voice, which could dart about the cellar at will, claimed to be on a divine mission to bring about the marriage: "'the parties must and would be joined,'" it declared, "'And what God hath joined together let no man put asunder.'"[19]   Accompanied by the glowing apparition, who floated over the frozen shoreline, Lydia Blaisdell and her father made a treacherous journey over the ice flows on the Taunton River on New Year's Day in 1800 to inform the family of George Butler that the ghost of his wife had returned with very specific demands.  A series of supernatural encounters then took place between the specter and those people closest in life to Nelly Butler, during which times the ghost displayed intimate knowledge of Nelly Butler's life while pursing single-mindedly the objective of bringing together the Blaisdell and Butler families.

A tempestuous courtship then followed for Lydia Blaisdell and George Butler at the bequest of the specter.  "The design of the marriage was made public," the earliest account states, "and round her [Lydia Blaisdell] increased the storm of accusation."[20]   The issue was not over the difference in the couple's age.  People were shocked to hear that the ghost of Nelly Butler had returned to orchestrate the proposed marriage.  Beginning to crumble under mounting stress and fear, Lydia tried to break off the engagement and flee south to York, Maine, where the Blaisdells had relatives.  "Thither she was determined to go, and made preparation for the voyage, that if possible she might find repose on some distant shore."[21] The spirit interrupted her plans; its "miraculous voice solemnly warned her, in the hearing of several witnesses, that her efforts were vain, and that her affliction would sail with her."[22]

The specter had its way. On the evening of May 28, 1800, the marriage took place on Butler's Point. The next day, in its most notorious manifestation, the phantom appeared to the newlyweds and prophesized that Lydia Blaisdell would bear but one child and die soon after. Of course, this was exactly how Nelly Butler had died. Strangely, the prophecy came true exactly ten months later, in March 1801, when sixteen-year-old Lydia Blaisdell died with her newborn in childbirth. For all intents and purposes, the first phase of the Nelly Butler hauntings had concluded on the evening of May 29, 1800, in a death curse.

The second period of the hauntings, comprising the spectacular appearances of August 1800, revealed totally different objectives. After disappearing for sixty-three days, the specter unexpectedly returned to the Blaisdell House on the first of August for a literal spree of supernatural encounters. During the specter's absence, the storm of controversy was on full boil, and many people spoke ill of the phantom, suspecting its origins in fraud or demonism. As if to dispel both rumors at the same time, the specter returned as a phantasmal preacher of the Lord, dazzling and overwhelming its spectators in a sheer display of its existence and power. The white lady spoke on religious subjects to large groups of people, almost forming an impromptu church in the black recesses of the Blaisdell cellar. On the night of August 8-9, 1800, more than thirty people crowded into the basement to witness the specter; the people even formed ranks through which the apparition passed back and forth five or six times. During the encounter, George Butler put his hand through the luminous form that resembled his dead wife. On the night of August 13-14, 1800, the specter culminated its manifestations by walking a mile with forty-eight people. Although most accounts of the apparition have it abruptly disappearing after this night, a personal account by Abraham Cummings dates the last confirmed sighting of the phantom to July 1806, in the fields of Waukeag Neck, in the town of Sorrento, near Sullivan.[23]

In both phases of its manifestations, the Nelly Butler apparition did not conform to the recorded behavior of a ghost. As stated by Rodger Anderson, a parapsychologist, "apparitions normally display an impoverished repertoire of behavior and do not appear even minimally sentient; the [...] [Nelly Butler] apparition, on the other hand, exhibited all the mental and emotional characteristics of a living human being."[24] In both its attempts to arrange a marriage, and to settle a host of scores, the strange specter was an entity peculiarly embedded in the affairs of the living. It seemed to be motivated by personal vengeance, vanity, and an inscrutable design as seen in arranging a marriage that would end in death. The Nelly Butler apparition displayed other bizarre attributes. While "[a]pparitions commonly appear unannounced and unexpected, [...] [this] apparition typically proclaimed its presence [...] sometimes predicting the time and place of her next visitation."[25] Extraordinary, indeed, was this ghost, which set appointments for its next appearance and then materialized to talk and sing alleluias for hours, yet this was the specter's mode of operation. "As if this were not in itself sufficiently bizarre," Rodger Anderson wrote, "the Specter would also invite her interlocutors to 'come and handle me.'"[26]

Due to its unconventional behavior, the Nelly Butler apparition was, from the very beginning, open to speculations of fraud. Quite simply, the ghost did not act like a ghost. While "authenticated instances of apparitions have been assiduously collected for nearly a century [...] none of these are even remotely comparable to the [...] [Nelly Butler] apparition."[27] Then there were other considerations that suggested deceitful practices. In the first phase of its manifestations, the phantom clearly seemed to advance the interests of young Lydia Blaisdell, who fought against the obstacles to her love for

Captain George Butler. Quite simply, it was too expedient for the ghost of his first wife then to appear and literally command the marriage. As stated in the earliest account, "It is a mixture of supernatural agency and artifice in the view of the opponents here—not because the least motion of the latter was ever really discovered, but because they judge (and feel capable of judging) that no case of marriage in any age of the world, since the *finis* of the Scriptures, can possibly require the interposition of an heavenly messenger."[28]

Theories of a hoax target Lydia as the deceiver working with a confederate, her only sister, Hannah, who was twenty at the time.[29] One young man, Paul Simpson, Jr., expressed "the opinion that the whole affair was a scheme contrived by [...] [Abner Blaisdell's] daughters, and nothing more."[30] Other people from the area shared Simpson's considerations. "These, with modern incredulity, now form the general opinion of the wise and unwise, the learned and unlearned, that this whole affair is mischief, and artifice, practiced by one or more of Abner Blaisdell's family, and particularly by the young woman, whose marriage was responsive to the prediction and direction of the specter."[31]

Skeptics of the Nelly Butler apparition found other attributes innately suspicious. To begin with, people wondered why the specter chose to haunt the Blaisdell House, and not the home where Nelly Butler had been born, or the house where she died as a young woman. Although the ghost appeared in other dwellings in the village, it never manifested itself in the Hooper House or on Butler's Point, with one possible exception—the wedding of Lydia Blaisdell and George Butler. The houses where the ghost appeared included James Miller's (located a half a mile from the Blaisdell House), Samuel Simpson's (a mile away), Josiah Simpson's (three miles away), and Abraham Cummings' (five miles away). Yet, the ghost did not materialize where one would most expect it, in the homes lived in by the actual Nelly Butler. "The fact that she [the ghost] instead chose a family with whom she had little earthly association appeared incongruous to a number of minds."[32]

Given the poor lighting of a candle or two, and the size and contents of the Blaisdell cellar, it was certainly possible for someone to be hiding there. Besides the entrance from inside the house (the East Room), the cellar contained two other forms of access: a bulkhead, or outside door, and at least one window, unglazed, with a wooden covering. In one documented case of fraud, a local man snuck into the cellar through the window and tried to impersonate the specter. This took place on the night of August 9, 1800, and the man in question was John Urann, a thirty-three year old cordwainer, who was quickly apprehended and thrown out. [33] The only other documented case of fraud took place later that same evening. When the company stood in the darkness of the cellar, some individuals present decided to imitate the spirit's rapping sounds. On this, Ambrose Simpson writes, "at length those who had no faith in its being a good spirit began to knock on his own account, and they caught one another by the arms while knocking, and they turned the affair into a spree."[34] Besides these cases of imposture, which occurred on one rowdy night (August 9th, a Saturday), no one has ever uncovered another instance of deception, despite the fact that the specter appeared on at least twenty-nine other occasions to more than a hundred people. As this and other evenings demonstrated, the Blaisdell cellar was subject to frequent searches by skeptical spectators.

Nevertheless, doubts in the spirit lingered. Some found it troubling that the ghostly voice customarily ordered the people to leave the cellar and return before it would manifest itself to them as glowing white phantom. "It was always she or one of the Blaisdells who always controlled the conditions of her appearance," Rodger Anderson pointed out, "never the witnesses. If people were in the cellar before the specter appeared, she would typically order them out so that they might 'come down in order' to see her phantasmal form."[35] While this is true for most of the appearances of the spirit, on at least eight occasions the phantom manifested itself with no warning or request for the people to leave and return. In some instances, like the night of August 9th, the spectators were disruptive, and the need for order would be necessary, not for fraud *per se*, but to conduct any kind of serious activity. As stated by Abraham Cummings, "The Specter was about to communicate to the assembly an important message. Could they enjoy the best advantage to hear and attend to it, while they were changing places—crowding and interrupting one another?"[36] Yet suspicions lived on regarding the conditions of the spiritualist encounters.

Questionable to some skeptics was the practice of conducing séances in complete darkness. Accounts concur that Abner Blaisdell habitually blew out the candle once everyone had assembled in the cellar, and a pitch-black darkness reigned until the appearance of the luminous wraith. Such a setting was conducive, many thought, to subterfuge. While all first-hand accounts agree that the apparition resembled Nelly Butler, the phantom chose to appear in different guises, sometimes wearing a cap and looking like Nelly Butler when she was alive and healthy, and other times wearing a shroud, or "winding sheet," and cradling her dead child in her arms.[37]

Reasonable as they may sound, theories of an outright hoax break down in several key areas. As stated by one early commentator, "A cellar, such as that was, is a place where a deceiver, imitating her realities, would find difficulty."[38] While an actor might indeed hide there, it was another thing entirely to make appearances in the very crowded space, much less talk for hours, without detection. Even if this were possible, the delusion would need to be extended to other houses and places, making the charade ever more complicated and perilous.

Ruling out an actor, however, was the shape-shifting capacity of the apparition. For those who witnessed the phantom, a fleeting, flickering quality characterized the image of the deceased woman. As pointed out by one witness, Jeremiah Bunker, the specter "appeared before us and disappeared several times. The personal shape, when it disappeared, first changed to a substance, without form, and then vanished in a moment where it was. And after a short space, the full personal form appeared again in a moment. These changes I observed several times."[39] Mary Gordon, a woman who had traveled to the Blaisdell House when it became famous throughout the land, had the following to say:

> At first the apparition was a mere mass of light, then grew into personal form, about as tall as myself. We stood in two ranks about four or five feet apart. Between these ranks she slowly passed and re-passed, so that any of us could have handled her. When she passed by me, her nearness was that of contact, so that, if there had been a substance, I should have certainly felt it. The glow of the apparition had a constant tremulous motion.[40]

On the substance of the luminous ghost, Paul Blaisdell testified that "The personal shape was all light, the particles of which had constant motion."[41]

Some people speculated that a primitive type of projector—a magic lantern—might have produced the image of the phantom. Yet this device also seems improbable given the constraints of a crowded cellar. "Now admit the possibility of a magic lantern," stated Abraham Cummings, "where did it move, and where stood the upright plane for the representation, when by the order of the Specter, the company of about twenty persons formed an ellipsis within which she passed and re-passed from end to end several times?"[42] A candle-lit projector simply cannot explain how the ghost could appear outside, as it did the night of August 13-14, 1800, and follow forty-eight people for a trip lasting a mile. "In all the appearances of the Specter," states the earliest account, "she was as white as the light, and this whiteness was as clear and visible in a dark cellar and dark night as when she appeared in the open field and in the open day."[43]

Also unaccountable was the spectral voice, which displayed strange properties. "Sometimes the inimitable voice would sound ten or twelve feet from us," testified Abner Blaisdell, "then close to our face, then again at a distance, and these changes were instantaneous."[44] Not only could the disembodied voice dart around the Blaisdell cellar with startling speed, but it sounded just like the voice of Nelly Butler, particularly on her deathbed. In her affidavit, Sally Wentworth recalled how she heard the spirit voice, "the sound of which brought fresh to mind that of my sister's voice, in an instant."[45] The ghost's voice was sometimes so loud that it shook the whole house while other times the voice sounded like it was receding through infinite depths of space. On the specter, a woman named Eunice Scammons testified, "I heard the voice of her praises sounding further and further from us for a considerable time before it entirely ceased."[46] Given the acoustic properties of the voice, some people speculated its source in ventriloquism with the aid of a tube that could distort the sound and lend to it a hollow quality. Although the voice "was plainly a different voice from that of Lydia Blaisdell, or any other that ever they had heard, necessity, the mother of invention, produced their hypothesis that Lydia Blaisdell was using some sounding instrument."[47] Even in the darkness of the cellar, Lydia would have been unable to project the spirit's voice without detection even if she were a skilled ventriloquist, much less could she use a "sounding instrument" and not be discovered. During séances, skeptics often stood close to Lydia, even holding her by the arm to prevent any deceitful practices.

What ruled out ventriloquism, if not all theories of outright fraud, was the strangest of phenomena—altered levels of perception coexisting at the same time and place. Regarding the ghostly voice, some people could hear and understand it distinctly, while others heard nothing at all, and some heard only a rubbed-out sound. "A ventriloquist might indeed speak there," wrote Abraham Cummings, "But how? Now so that a part of the company shall hear and understand distinctly, while the other part with the advantages of hearing everyway equal, and giving equal attention, shall not understand a single word."[48]

The specter's ability to manipulate sense perception extended from its voice to its actual appearance as an intensely white form of a woman. The specter promised to be visible only to those who chose to see it. Accordingly, the ghost was invisible to anyone who wished—either secretly or publicly—to avoid seeing it. For example, Sarah Simpson attended one séance and reported that "I was soon after informed, that the spirit was about to appear [...]. I went with the rest, but prayed that I might not see her. She had promised that none should see her but those who desired it. Accordingly, I did not see her, though I looked directly before me, where they said that she was."[49]

It is difficult to imagine how anyone could have contrived the apparition through an actor, a projector, or any other mechanical means to achieve such an effect. "Such was the various experience of the people on these occasions. Some of them heard and understood plainly, but saw nothing; others heard a voice, but no speaking; others again saw a light, but no person while they had no impediments natural or accidental; yet far the greater number heard the words distinctly, and clearly saw a personal form. And the very same persons [...] who had clearly seen and understood at the previous interview, could now only see a light and hear a sound."[50]

In addition to the supernatural encounters already described, the ghost also called for the re-interment of Nelly Butler's child. The purpose of digging up the baby's grave was to move its contents closer to the remains of Nelly Butler so "that the child would rise at her right hand at the last day."[51] Eighty people assembled for the event, which probably took place in the autumn after the apparition's spectacular finale in mid-August 1800.[52] The setting was Butler's Point, in Franklin, the location of Nelly's grave and that of her child. As stated in a letter by Abraham Cummings, "This [ceremony] was not a mere accident, but a deliberate and public transaction, appropriated by no other pretence of any reason, but the mere order of the specter. [...] The whole affair was considered by mankind in general as a solemn, mysterious parade, without any apparent consequence of injury or utility."[53]

When arguments for outright fraud break down, theories of mass hallucination step in to explain the Nelly Butler hauntings. "Scores of people standing for hours in a pitch-black cellar waiting for a phantom to appear, all the while being warned by a disembodied voice to repent lest they be forever damned, provides a perfect setting for a visionary epidemic."[54] Thus wrote Rodger Anderson, who included in his argument for a mass delusion the fact that the specter appeared "only to those 'who had a desire to see her,' which was in accord with her promise that 'none should see her but those who desired it.' If these and similar statements can be credited, it would appear that the bodily presence of the specter was hallucinatory in nature."[55] This perhaps would explain the shape-shifting appearance of the specter in its various manifestations.

While misperception no doubt influenced the Nelly Butler hauntings, theories of mass hallucination also have trouble explaining particular features of the events. The argument depends to a large extent on the susceptibility of the people who witnessed the apparition. Some individuals in the Blaisdell cellar certainly believed the place was haunted, and these people expected to see to the apparition of Nelly Butler at any moment. But the majority of those present were frankly skeptical, if not downright hostile in their suspicions of being hoaxed. These individuals did not encounter what they expected to find, an actor dressed up like Nelly Butler, or a ventriloquist hiding in a cider barrel. Instead, they witnessed the shape-shifting form of a woman radiating an intense light.

The intensely luminescent quality of the specter is particularly difficult to explain as a mass delusion. When the phantom approached its spectators in the Blaisdell cellar, they "appeared to be immersed in her radiance so that [...] [they] appeared white and shining like the apparition."[56] In her affidavit, Abigail Abbott stated emphatically that "the specter gave so much light that we could see other persons and other things in the cellar, which we could not see before her appearance, nor afterwards."[57] Circumstances such as these would seem to exceed the capacity of a mass hallucination. To date, there have been no studies attempting to explain the Nelly Butler hauntings in terms of hallucinations triggered by physical causes like encephalitis, ergot poisoning, or psychotropic drugs.

Given its sensational manifestations, the specter left its skeptics confounded, but the controversy only deepened at the time of the events. Suspicions of demonism and satanic witchcraft soon overshadowed the proceedings. "Since the 'Salem Witchcraft' nothing of a local nature has created such a furor of excitement, in this vicinity as the, so called 'Blaisdell Spirit' affair, which occurred in Sullivan, A.D. 1800," wrote Thomas Foss.[58] "The favorite theory of the dissenters was that, while the wraith of the dead woman resembled her exactly it must have been a simulacrum fashioned by the Devil. In so doing, of course, Satan was up to no good."[59] While Nelly Butler's parents—David and Joanna Hooper—were staunch believers in the apparition, and so was George Butler—at least up to the death of Lydia Blaisdell—an opposing faction was deeply distrustful of the specter. This group considered the apparition to be a demon or "damned spirit."[60]

One of the most prominent detractors of the specter was Sally Wentworth, the sister of Nelly Butler. On January 3rd, Sally Wentworth visited the Blaisdell House, heard the spirit's voice, but could not comprehend its words. Later that day in the East Room she overheard the phantom speaking in the cellar and unexpectedly understood its words, which included its statement, "'I am the voice of one crying in the wilderness.'"[61] In the testimony she submitted, Sally Wentworth stated that "From that time I cleared Lydia as to the voice, and accused the devil." [62] Summing up her opinion, Sally Wentworth was the first to propose the theory that "some evil spirit [...] [did] personate my sister."[63]

A growing number of people who had witnessed the ghost at the Blaisdell House came to share Sally Wentworth's point of view. It was this opinion that the specter sought openly to discredit in August 1800, during the second phase of the hauntings. At this time, the specter summoned some of its most outspoken critics, such as Paul Simpson, James Miller, and Sally Wentworth. As events in the community took a nasty turn with accusations of demonism, the specter reinvented itself as a ghostly preacher interspersing religious platitudes with sensational shows of supernatural powers. "In some old fashioned minds," wrote Abraham Cummings of the specter, "her familiar conversation may excite the suspicion of necromancy and divination, by a *familiar* spirit, so plainly forbidden in the Law of Moses: and then doubtless Lydia Blaisdell must bear the accusation."[64] According to local lore, the apparition was a demonic entity summoned by Lydia Blaisdell to actualize her romantic aspirations. Conjuring spirits would have had a special appeal to young Lydia, desperate in her attachments. Even before the hauntings commenced, she was described as "one who never gave the least evidence of piety."[65] Of course, no one thought Lydia would want to raise the actual ghost of Nelly Butler. But a spirit that could take on the appearance of that woman would well suit her purposes. Looking like the deceased and much-beloved first wife, a matchmaking specter would possess considerable authority.

Some modern parapsychologists share the suspicions of Lydia's contemporaries that the ghost was not the spirit of Nelly Butler but rather a summoned entity of supernatural origin. After studying the case, Muriel Roll wrote that "several features of the case suggest that Lydia was a medium and that the apparition and other phenomena originated with her. One of them is her frequent physical proximity to the occurrences. [...] There are [also] several references to Lydia's depleted energy during the meetings, again pointing to her involvement."[66] Conjuring spirits also explained, for Muriel Roll, the pattern of supernatural encounters, in both the first and second phases in the history of the hauntings. "Since Lydia and the captain were married on May 28th, this event and the fact that it constituted a confirmation of the Specter's prediction could be associated with the May clustering. [...] The accumulating pressures of the accusations and the need to disprove them might account for the increased number of appearances in August."[67] Roll's argument cannot account for the spirit's manifestations when Lydia Blaisdell was not present—encounters that may include group sightings in the first week of August 1800 as well as an appearance five years after Lydia's death.[68] Yet numerous features in the Nelly Butler hauntings involve a conscious intent to raise a spirit. These included a gathering in the darkness, a formal summoning, and a communion with a supernatural entity.

A learned man and traveling evangelist, Abraham Cummings published the original history of the Nelly Butler hauntings in 1826 in a work entitled *Immortality Proved by the Testimony of Sense: in Which Is Considered the Doctrine of Spectres, and the Existence of a Particular Spectre.* This work included a remarkable number of eye-witness testimonies and depositions transcribed by Cummings in late August 1800.

Cummings stayed with his family in a number of coastal Maine communities where he provided ministerial duties for periods of time. Church records from Sullivan, Maine, reveal that Cummings was preaching and living in the area from 1799-1803. This period of time was broken by six months in 1800, when Cummings was in Bucksport, Maine, where he founded a Baptist church. Abraham Cummings was thus absent for the bulk of the hauntings, since he left Sullivan sometime in January 1800 and returned in August just after the climax of the spirit's manifestations. No accounts from this period refer to Cummings being present at spiritualist encounters at the Blaisdell House.

Despite his absence from the area during the key events, Abraham Cummings witnessed the Nelly Butler apparition on two separate occasions. Based on a first-person footnote that he added to the testimony of Captain Paul Simpson, Cummings heard the specter speak on January 3, 1800. He appears to have left unimpressed by its message. At one point in time, the hollow, disembodied voice declared in anger, "'I am not to be trifled with. I am not to be trifled with. I am not to be trifled with. Peace, peace, peace.'"[69] On this Abraham Cummings wrote, "These enigmatical warnings were some of the first words which the voice uttered, and they appeared strange to us all. They appeared to be void of instruction, impertinent, and utterly inapplicable to anything which was seen, remembered, or expected among us. None were then trifling with her; all wondered, and many were solemnized. Nor was there any remarkable contention among us."[70] Cummings was also disturbed by the ghost's preference for the cellar of the house. Of the specter, he wrote for that day, "Her speaking so much in a by-place [a cellar] separate from the common dwelling of man, like John in the wilderness, has offended us."[71] Swept up in the whirlwind of religious revivalism at the period and then, at the end of January, faced with moving his small family, Abraham Cummings devoted little thought to the specter he had heard in the Blaisdell cellar, but he filed the experience away for later reflection. He returned in August, amazed by the mass sightings of the ghost that he had largely missed. In reflecting on the January 3rd encounter, he found the spirit's words to be prophetic, referring to the ridicule and controversy that had come to surround the strange apparition and its objectives in the world of the living.

Abraham Cummings' second encounter with the specter left a most profound impact on the man. In the last recorded sighting of the Nelly Butler apparition, the ghost appeared unexpectedly in July 1806, long after the hauntings had become legend. The encounter took place outside, in a field "twelve rods distance from the house," located on Waukeag Neck, where Abraham Cummings was staying with his family.[72] Cummings reported that "in the evening I was informed by two persons that they had just seen the Specter in the field."[73] Believing them to be mistaken, he went out shortly afterwards. "I saw there, as I supposed, one of the white rocks," he wrote, and "This confirmed my opinion of their specter, and I paid no more attention to it. Three minutes after, I accidentally looked in the same direction, and the white rock was in the air, its form a complete globe, white with a tincture of red, like the damask rose, and its diameter about two feet."[74] As he started toward the luminous orb, "it came to me from the distance of eleven rods, as quick as lightening, and instantly assumed a personal form with a female dress."[75] At first the apparition was no taller than a little girl. "While I looked upon her," wrote Cummings, "I said in my mind, 'You are not tall enough for the woman who has so frequently appeared among us.' Immediately she grew up as large and as tall as I considered that woman to be.'"[76] Stricken with amazement, Abraham Cummings never actually spoke to the apparition. Nevertheless, the encounter left such a deep impression on the man that he would spend his last days recording the history of the Nelly Butler hauntings.

Circumstances conspired to make Abraham Cummings the eventual champion of the specter. Although he felt initial fear when he encountered the ghost, he claimed that he also experienced "ineffable pleasure."[77] Close ties with people like Abner Blaisdell and George Butler predisposed him to believe in the spirit and sympathize with its claims. This prompted Cummings to cast himself into the center of the debates surrounding the phantom. Yet a deeper motive inspired him to take up the gauntlet, claiming that the specter was both genuine and benevolent. At the time, Cummings was intensely battling the skeptical legacy of the Enlightenment. Most threatening for Cummings was the philosophical claim of materialism that there is no soul. The unprecedented nature of the Nelly Butler hauntings promised to vanquish this claim once and for all. "The result of this whole inquiry," wrote Cummings, referring to the history of the hauntings, "is that of consolation. Our death will not be total. Our souls will survive our bodies."[78] Witnessed by more than a hundred people in sensational manifestations that confounded skeptics, the whole story of the Nelly Butler hauntings was, for Cummings, like "apples of gold and pictures of silver."[79]

For centuries the whole story of the Nelly Butler hauntings has been buried in virtual obscurity. It is the equivalent of a witch hunt that had somehow eluded future historians and writers. The original account by Abraham Cummings is an extremely rare text. Including both the 1826 and 1859 editions, only ten libraries worldwide own either copy. Because of the inaccessibility of the original account, the story has never received the attention it deserves, writers perpetuate significant errors to the present day, and retellings pass over much of the narrative's complexity. The most grievous error in retellings situates the events in the town of Machiasport, Maine, fifty miles away from their true location in

Sullivan. This mistake began in 1949, when William Oliver Stevens rediscovered the story of the Nelly Butler hauntings. The original 1826 edition is notoriously sparse in its place references. This caused the publisher J.L. Lovell to attach a note to the title page of the second edition, specifying "By phenomena that were witnessed by hundreds in the town of Sullivan, Maine, in the year 1800." Working with the earlier edition, William Oliver Stevens missed the buried references to Sullivan and was the first to claim that the "ghost appeared in a Maine seaport village, which, one may guess from internal evidence, must have been near Machiasport."[80] Stevens may have chosen Machiasport since Hoopers settled there, and Nelly Butler's maiden name was Eleanor Hooper. But more likely, the source of the error was a simple miscalculation. The original account made it clear that York was 200 miles south of the story's setting, and Stevens may have overestimated the distance. At any rate, the mistaken location lives on, in websites and in recent publications, since writers rarely refer back to the original source. Exacerbating the inaccessibility of this source is the organization of Cummings, who buried the first-hand accounts. He began and ended his work in long philosophical reflections on immortality. This dense, 18th century prose is extremely tedious for modern readers and needlessly delays them from engaging with the complexities of the apparition's appearances and historical responses.

Primary sources on the Nelly Butler hauntings come from *Immortality Proved by the Testimony of Sense* by Abraham Cummings. Digitally transcribing these documents involved a careful comparison with the second, and last, edition from 1859 held in the Maine State Museum. All efforts have been taken to present original documents in their accuracy and entirety, but some alterations have been done for sake of clarity, usage, and presentation. For the most part, individuals in the original account appear only by title and last name (e.g. Mrs. Butler, Captain Simpson). In this edition, titles have been retained only for the name of a testimony; thereafter, individuals appear in the accounts by their first and last names. This avoids confusion since many individuals have the same last name. Antiquated spelling and punctuation have been updated with one exception—the capitalization of the words "Specter" or "Spirit" whenever they refer to the Nelly Butler apparition. This is a notable motif in the original sources and thus retained.

The Nelly Butler hauntings are exceptional in the record they contain regarding one of the most cryptic events in Early America. Written in the simple language of the time, the letters, depositions, and testimonies that comprise the primary documents are surprisingly accessible to modern readers. Of course, the story contains a number of elements that give it a timeless appeal: supernatural encounters, proof of an afterlife, a love triangle between the living and the dead, and a storm of controversy that refuses to go away. For the apparition known as Nelly Butler orchestrated a marriage, a death, and a sensation unmatched to the present day. The hauntings remain one of the great mysteries of history.

—Marcus LiBrizzi
  Machiasport, Maine, June 13, 2010

❀❀❀

## LETTERS BY ABRAHAM CUMMINGS

❀❀❀

Abraham Cummings was a man steeped in both arcane mysticism and the philosophy of the Enlightenment. In 1776, he received his A.M. degree from Brown University, known at the time as Rhode Island College.[1] He was described as being "very much alive to the spiritual and unseen,"[2] and as having "unconventional ideas for a Baptist minister. One of his unorthodox beliefs was his conviction of the reality of the world of spirits and of their nearness to human life."[3] In addition to his account of the Nelly Butler hauntings, he published other books on mysticism and the supernatural. *Spirits and Phantasms* and *The Millennium* both appeared in 1797.[4] In 1812, Cummings wrote *Contemplations on the Cherubim*.[5] The man also saw some of his sermons published, including one he delivered in Sullivan in 1799, ironically on the anniversary of Nelly Butler's birth, April 25th. The sermon, entitled "The Present Times Perilous," made no reference to Nelly Butler; instead, it described signs that foretold the end of the world.

Cummings wrote the original history of the Nelly Butler hauntings in a work entitled *Immortality Proved by the Testimony of Sense: in Which Is Considered the Doctrine of Spectres, and the Existence of a Particular Spectre.* The book was printed in 1826 and republished in 1859. At the core of this book are six letters written by Cummings on the mysterious and sensational series of events that took place in Downeast Maine in 1799-1800. Cummings claims that his letters are "In reply to a friend who had expressed his desire and that of others that the account of the Specter might not be made public." [6] The following letters thus imply a skeptical reader.

# LETTER I
## *On the Appearance, Voice, and Disposition of the Specter*

My Dear Sir, In our last interview, you favored me with the suspense of your judgment with regard to the Specter, which has produced so much altercation in this part of the land.

I am therefore encouraged to ask your further attention to this affair, contemptible as it must appear, if you believe but a part of the misrepresentation now propagated. These, with modern incredulity, now form the general opinion of the wise and unwise, the learned and unlearned, that this whole affair is mischief, and artifice, practiced by one or more of Abner Blaisdell's family, and particularly by the young woman, whose marriage was responsive to the prediction and direction of the Specter. Thus stands the vision of Hosea in the view of our Deists.[7] They consider it a thousand times more probable that the good man was somehow or other deceived by those licentious women, than that he ever received such direction from the invisible world. Now while my own opinion is entirely the reverse—while I view that family and their neighbors who vindicate them as unjustly censured—shall I appear the *sang froid* spectator? Perish rather my own reputation with theirs.

But this notwithstanding, dear sir, you will not fail to mention the ardent sensations of gratitude and esteem which I entertain for those pious and judicious persons who have expressed their generous anxiety for my character and usefulness.

It is not so much the matter or style of the pious discourse of the Specter which demands our attention, as the enquiry whether there was any Specter or not. She taught the same truth which we find in our Bible. She proclaimed no new doctrine. Had she done this, it would have occasioned a great objection against her.[8] She exhorted the young people to read the Bible as their sure guide to eternal life. And her requirements were defended by the Scriptures whenever the propriety of any of them was doubted, to show that her directions agreed with the law and the testimony.

In the style of her discourse, there was nothing of elegance or sublimity, more or less than we observe among common people in that pious and familiar conversation in which passages of Scripture are frequently introduced.

This, they say, is a great objection: a person from the invisible state would never have conversed with the people in such an ordinary style. But had she excelled in the *elegant* or *sublime*, objection would not have been silent. It would have been said that she was not the person she professed to be, for the employment of that person had never been the study of Sheridan or Longinus: on earth she was below it, in heaven above it.[9] The Specter came not with the excellency of speech, which man teaches, nor with the sublimity of those prophecies which describe the rise and ruin of empires, for empires were not her subject, and there was perfect propriety in her using such language as would subserve two of her designs: which were to manifest who she was, and to render herself as familiar as possible to those common people with whom she conversed. Accordingly, her mention of certain articles of property which she had left was by no means an ultimate design, as she herself declared, but this, and her reasonable disposal of them, were more clearly to convince her family that she had been their daughter and sister. For the same reason the features of her face were observed to be like those of the person she professed to be, by some who knew her in her lifetime. And though her voice had no indication of breath and was inimitably distinct from any voice of the living, yet it had the same sound which she had uttered in her last hours, as they, who attended her in her last sickness have testified. Sometimes a part of the company could understand her words without the least difficulty, while others with advantages of hearing, everyway equal, perceived only a sound, without the least articulation whatever. Thus the men who were with Paul at the time of his conversion, heard a voice, but saw no man, and they saw the light, but heard not the articulate voice of the speaker.[10]

Such was the various experience of the people on these occasions. Some of them heard and understood plainly, but saw nothing; others heard a voice, but no speaking voice; others again saw a light, but no person while they had no impediments natural or accidental; yet far the greater number heard the words distinctly, and clearly saw a personal form. And the very same persons, who could not see, nor hear intelligibly at one time, would at another time, and even at a greater distance see, hear, and understand without the least difficulty—while others of the company, who had clearly seen and understood at the previous interview, could now only see a light and hear a sound.

It was to render herself familiar that she frequently introduced herself, as we do, by the token of knocking.

When Peter knocked at the house of Mary, the disciples thought it was his angel, that is to say, they thought that a spirit might come to the house and knock.[11] They more easily believed that a spirit was at the door, than that Peter had escaped from prison. We should in this age more easily believe the contrary. But the disciples were no philosophers.

For the same reason she endeavored to dispel the fears of those who conversed with her. "Do not be afraid," she would say. "I have not come to hurt you. You need not be afraid at all." Utterly opposite, you observe, to the conduct of those who personate apparitions. They generally aim to keep their dupes in fear and at a convenient distance.

So the angel addressed the shepherds, "Fear not."[12] "I do not stand too near you, do I?" said a person unsuspected. "No," was the reply. "Stand as near as you please."

Hence also the reason why she did not commonly begin to speak, till she was addressed. I say, *commonly*, for there were some exceptions. The voice of a ghost responsive is not so unexpected, and, of course, not so suddenly terrific as the same voice would be without previous address. This may serve to remove that objection of the *Encyclopedia*: "It is an odd circumstance," say they, "that ghosts have no power to speak till they are addressed."[13] But this odd circumstance is not occasioned by their want of power, but by their tenderness for the persons who receive their messages. This was the very reason she once expressly gave for not speaking where she once appeared. Hence we may, if we choose, see one reason why she spoke so frequently in the cellar. It is easy to see, if we choose, that the idea of a Specter coming into the room where the family commonly resided for labor, sleep, or other refreshment was distressing to them: for this was their refuge, their place of retreat. Accordingly when, upon a certain day, she appeared among them in one of the lower rooms, they all left the house.[14] The Specter, therefore, out of tenderness to them, *commonly*, though not always, conversed in the cellar, that they might seem to have a place of retreat. The next question is, why then did she not commonly speak in one of the chambers or in the open field? But the chambers were the apartments of repose, and the field was inconvenient by the weather. She did, however, sometimes speak in the chambers, and in the lower rooms, and in other houses of the neighborhood, and several times in the open field.

A cellar, such as that was, is a place where deceivers, imitating her realities would find difficulty. A ventriloquist might indeed speak there. But how? Not so that a part of the company shall hear and understand distinctly, while the other part with advantages of hearing everyway equal, and giving equal attention, shall not understand a single word. If a ventriloquist could perform this, we should have known it before this time.

No white garments can appear white in a dark cellar at midnight, and suppose any lucid substance could have been used, then, when it first appeared a mere shapeless mass, who formed it in a moment into personal shape, face, and features? Who caused it to speak and desired to be handled? And when this desire was complied with, why did not the hand undeceive the eyes? Now admit the possibility of a magic lantern, where did it move, and where stood the upright plane for the representation, when by the order of the Specter, the company of about twenty persons formed an ellipsis within which she passed and re-passed from end to end several times? You must inform me too how some eyes saw the form so clearly, while others, with advantages of sight every way equal, saw nothing.

However, it is not even pretended that any such mediums of delusion were ever seen here.

For an argument which vindicates this conduct of the Specter still more, I am indebted to Dugald Stewart. "It appears to me to be no slight confirmation of these remarks," says he, "that, although in the dark, the illusions of imagination are much more liable to be mistaken for realities, than when their momentary effects on the belief are continually checked and corrected by the objects which the light of day presents to our perception; yet even total darkness is not so alarming to a person impressed with vulgar stories of apparitions, as a faint and doubtful twilight, which affords to the conceptions an opportunity of fixing and prolonging their existence by attaching themselves to something which is obscurely exhibited to the sight."[15] Hence it follows, that in a dark cellar at midnight, a person was not so much exposed to deception, either by his own imagination, or by the artifice of others, as if there had been some degree of light. Had the ghost been wholly confined to a cellar, kitchen, or garret, or even to all these, the objection would appear more plausible, but this was by no means the case.

Accompanied by two persons she walked, or rather moved in elevation from the ground, nearly two miles, discoursing with them as she went along.[16] "For what purpose?" you ask. Doubtless an important one. But to what purpose could I tell you while you reject the possibility of it for any purpose?

This little journey was soon published through the town but was no more believed than this luminous age now believes the writer. What was the consequence? "Go," said the Specter, "to one of those two persons. Collect all those in the neighborhood who give the best evidence of piety and veracity. Let them hear and see, for they will tell the truth." He complied, and fifty people were convened at the time and place appointed for the interview.[17]

After conversing with them several hours on the most serious topics, by which they were exceedingly affected and delighted, she reminded them of their credulity, and informed them that if they would walk on two and two in the solemn order observed at a funeral, she would walk with them, accompanied by one of those persons who had accompanied her before, for evidence that they might have declared the truth. The company complied, and walked with her about half a mile in the manner now described.[18]

But after all, I hear you inquire, "*admitting that the whole affair is genuine and free from illusion, how can the belief of it become beneficial to me and others?*"

But certainly truth is better that error. And do we know that this truth will never be wanted hereafter, for purposes which do not at present appear? Do you know how soon your own or other families may suffer unjust reproach, like the family and vicinity who are now so liberally censured? Do we know the length and weight of the chain of which this link is a part?

The Scriptures teach the doctrine of the separate state, and oppose materialism. What then? Is the evidence of Scripture injured by other evidence declaring the same truth and urging the study of the Scriptures, as our sure guide to eternal life? The ancient medals and other monuments of antiquity, which afford so much rational entertainment for the curious, never diminish in their eyes the evidence of value of the Roman, Grecian, or Egyptian history. Why then should this medal before us diminish in our eyes the value of the Scriptures? What distinction of men are they who stand most secure from the peril of illusion by the superstitious belief of specters? Speak, ye Illuminees! ye Paines, who keep no Bible![19]

# LETTER II
## THE CIRCUMSTANCES OF THE MARRIAGE RELATED IS VINDICATION OF LYDIA BLAISDELL AND OTHERS

Dear Sir, To compare great things with small, the unbelieving Jews, who heard and saw the first Christian miracles to be really such, viewing them as the effects of magic or some other secret influence of Satan—but modern infidels say they were no miracles at all—so the opponents of the Specter in this place, who have heard and seen, generally allow that the performances of the ghost were miraculous, but accomplished by evil agency, while distant opponents pronounce the whole an artifice.

Thus distance of place has occasioned the same variations among the opponents of the Specter, as distance of time among the opponents of Christianity. By this comparison you must not imagine that I have reference to criminality, but my design is to show that the friends and foes of the Specter in this place are both opposed by those distant people who pronounce the whole an artifice. It is a mixture of supernatural agency and artifice in the view of the opponents here —not because the least motion of the latter was ever really discovered, but because they judge (and feel capable of judging) that no case of marriage in any age of the world, since the *finis* of the Scriptures, can possibly require the interposition of a heavenly messenger.[20]

We, on the contrary, are so poorly qualified to determine how the world ought to be governed that we know not what events should take place by ordinary means, or what by extraordinary means, and therefore we know not but there might be such a circumstance in some place or period of the world.

We are too as much at a loss to account for the advent of an evil angel singing alleluias, in order to join a couple mutually attached in a relation which is honorable in all, as to account for the advent of a holy angel for the same purpose.

It is necessary, without all doubt, that such an extraordinary dispensation should be connected with an important consequence and a special reason why it took place. But it is not necessary that this consequence and reason should at present be universally known, though they certainly will be known hereafter, and probably in part to many in this world. The performances of the ghost are so connected with other events of Providence as to form a connected whole, the beauty of which cannot be known even in part without much examination.

The Specter had a number of extraordinary messages, of which the marriage was but one, and that a subordinate one, and accordingly did produce extraordinary credentials.

The very first notices of anything unaccountable were given at the time when Lydia Blaisdell, the supposed authoress of the whole delusion, was at the point of death, by a disease which soon became external and proved its reality. Was that the time for her to commence the enterprise for a husband, when she must have been under the greatest disadvantage for the prosecution of it, and when there was no rational explanation that she would ever need a husband?

About twenty-four hours after her marriage, the Specter foretold that she would become the parent of one child and then die.[21] For what purpose *could* she, or any person for her, contrive this prediction and its fulfillment? Her walk of two miles in company with the Specter and her father was undertaken with great reluctance, if anything could be known by the correspondence of words and behavior.[22] But the small voice of one who had made the house tremble informed them by a message that lives were in danger, if they refused. By the same voice the Scripture was quoted to show that her direction was not inconsistent with it. What could have been done in this case more than was done by the most pious or prudent on earth? The Scriptures were consulted. The family prayed together, that, if there was deception in this extraordinary injunction, the Lord would make it known to them, and that, if the cause was of God, they might be preserved. For the storm, the evening, and especially the weakness of the ice, had rendered the way difficult and very perilous. When to these considerations we add the grievous offence and explicit repulse, which the whole family had that day received from the person to whom her father was, out of her hearing, to communicate the message, we cannot admit the idea of artifice in Lydia Blaisdell, without detaching from her all fear of danger—all sense of resentment—all respect due from a child to the parent—all rationality of conduct, and all consistency of character.[23]

But further, the greatest and most conspicuous of these miracles appeared after the marriage. Could she, would she, or any person for her, perform these impossibles to obtain a purpose which was obtained already? But admitting the plea for a minute, and but a minute, that they were possibles intended to establish the farce and multiply dupes for the preservation of character, a question then urges incessantly: *For what purpose was the child dug up and buried in another grave?*[24] This was not a mere accident, but a deliberate and public transaction, appropriated by no *pretence* of any reason, but the mere order of the Specter. Eighty people from four different towns were assembled and offered prayer to the Supreme Being on this occasion, and all by the direction of the ghost, declaring that the child would rise at her right hand at the last day. This was horrid wickedness in the ghost, if she was only such by profession. And our opponents must, for their own sakes, allow that she possessed a great degree of subtlety, if not of wisdom, since for twenty-six years past they have for the most part scarcely ventured to conjecture, much less to prove, who she was—though by their own acknowledgment she has talked among twenty of them, from time to time, within a foot of their faces.

Doubtless then some special design was concealed in this rare transaction. What was it? The continuation and extension of the fraud? No, for she must have known that the least of those miracles already exhibited would better answer this purpose were it now presented only before a small part of these eighty people. But the re-interment was not connected with even the pretense of miracle. What was the consequent impression on the minds of mankind? Just what any person with half an eye would easily foresee. It was such as rendered Lydia Blaisdell's character, in the eye of mankind, neither better nor worse. What could she think to gain or lose in character or anything else, whether that other woman's child rested in its first grave, or in another about thirty feet from it? The whole affair was considered by mankind in general as a solemn, mysterious parade, without any apparent consequence of injury or utility.

But this practical oath, as already shown, was not without design. What was it? Was it to convince the assembly *at that time*, that Abner Blaisdell and George Butler, who acted the most distinguished and solemn part in it, believed the Specter and her performance to be realities? No, for this they were completely convinced already. The question, therefore, with our opponents stands unresolved. When we consider too the inimitable sound of the voice, most nearly resembling the dying voice of George Butler's first wife, at certain times, and how often the ghost has appeared since Nelly Butler's death, all suspicion of artifice must be utterly groundless, and cannot be indulged by those who love their neighbors as themselves, and exercise that constant tenderness for their characters which the gospel requires.

It has been objected against the Specter that, in obtaining parental approbation, the mothers were not sufficiently respected.[25] But as the husband and wife are one, the message to the father was virtually sent to the mother. It was necessary in this case that three families should be consulted by the Spirit: that which had been her own family and those of the parties.

But with whom began this consultation? Not with Eve, like that of the devil. She did not, like a deceiver, first frighten and convince the timorous sex that they might assist her, either to delude or afflict their husbands. No, her conduct was fair and aboveboard. Her first application was to the fathers of these families. What was it? Certainly not that which is recommended by the *Encyclopedia* and the ballad poem, but that of deliberation. She at first neither appeared nor spoke to them immediately to frighten them into compliance at once, but as she had dealt with the son,[26] so she dealt with the fathers. She sent messages to them.

By this fair mode of conduct, they had opportunity to reflect, to exercise reason—to consult one another, and to watch and pray against deception. Her first message, sent only to the two fathers of this couple, contained that passage in Mark 10: 2 to 9, by which they might learn that—as the condition of ancient Israel at a certain time, required a precept with respect to marriage, somewhat distinct from the common law, which had existed from the beginning—so now the condition of this little branch of society might, for aught they knew, required a precept with respect to marriage, somewhat distinct from the common regulation, which had obtained from the beginning, though not contrary to it, even as a by-law may be consistent with the public code.

Such, she declared, was the precept now revealed for the particular regulation of those families, and her proofs to be produced, were her miracles. A strange, unexpected, unheard of message indeed! But not more strange, unexpected, or unheard of, than the credentials. By this precept she declared the parties must and would be joined. "And what God hath joined together let not man put asunder."

The father of the young lady, who had ever been most obstinately opposed to this connection, by whose means it had been once interrupted already, and who was no less capable than the other of discovering imposition, and ever watchful against it, was the first who obtained conviction. Him the Specter sent to the other father (Moses Butler) and his son to declare this conviction, and that the latter must conduct accordingly. The response was repulse, and he returned.

By the same extraordinary counsel, after praying and reading for light, he went again, and his daughter with him, crying and wringing her hands. After they had proceeded a small distance, they were accompanied by the Specter the rest of the way, whose delightful voice uttering expressions full of love and tenderness, consoled the daughter as they went along.[27] This prepared her for acquiescence when coming to the house of the Specter, as decency required, directed, that, while the daughter should tarry with her abroad, the father should go in and tell Moses Butler's family that the Specter had come with them, and that, if they chose a miracle for further confirmation, it should be granted.

After Moses Butler had preformed this, they invited the daughter to come in, and the question of suspicion being proposed, she solemnly protested that, if there was mischief in hand, she was as ignorant of it as they were.[28]

Here we see what abundant opportunity was given them to deliberate and consider for themselves in what way they would choose to be convinced—whether by miracle or common Providence.

Message, protestation, and miracle being rejected, Abner Blaisdell and his daughter returned without delay, but had no sooner reached home then a new order from the Specter, consistent with Scripture, required that David Hooper, who had been her father, and who lived about six miles off, should be conducted here the next morning.[29]

We now return to Moses Butler's family, not to see miracles, but their confirmation by the voice of common Providence.

After Abner Blaisdell and his daughter had left them, his conduct was naturally the subject of their discussion, and the more they reasoned, the more unaccountable it appeared. His notorious and inflexible opposition to this connection, which had continued several years, rendered him the most unlikely person in the world to pass a river, now the brink of death, for such a purpose.[30]  Their result was the necessity of further advice, and they unanimously chose David Hooper, the young gentleman's father-in-law, as the person best qualified to give it.  Accordingly, the son, George Butler, went the next morning to consult with him on this affair, but to his great surprise found himself intercepted by messengers sent by the ghost for the same purpose, who had just finished their business with success.[31]  George Butler asked what he should do. "The case is such," said David Hooper, "that I can have no advice to give."

David Hooper, according to his promise, went off with the messengers, discoursed with the Specter, and by the tokens which she gave him, identified his daughter.

After the deliberation of several days, he, by the desire of the Specter, went to Moses Butler's family, declared his conviction, and closed the message by solemn exhortation.[32]  Thus was the very man, whose advice they had preferred to a miracle, qualified by the Specter to give it.

But to recede:  David Hooper's interview with the Spirit at Abner Blaisdell's house was immediately succeeded by the arrival of George Butler there.  He soon acquired evidence that the Spirit was that of his deceased wife and declared that her will was his.

But now to what purpose were all this labor and all these messages?  For Lydia Blaisdell was then asked if the same was her will?   The reply was categorical and indignant, the purport of which was, that if she must die for her refusal, she desired to submit—that servile attentions, however miraculous the compulsion, would afford no satisfaction to her—that her trials were already intolerable by those false and wicked calumnies, which her compliance would now invigorate and render her life more bitter than death.   That her attachment to his person was peculiar, she did not deny, but his credulous attention to these calumnies had rendered his society a burden.[33] At length, however, George Butler's unreserved and honorable confession, and his renewed assurances that his *own* will was his, as well as that of his deceased wife, did, with the words of the Specter prevail.

The design of marriage was made public, and round her increased the storm of accusation abroad, and opposition at home.   For, though her father had constant and unwavering conviction that the precept was from heaven, it was only at certain intervals that he enjoyed the least degree of reconcilement, and it must not be concealed that George Butler received very ill treatment from him.

Worn out by unjust reproaches abroad and these vexations at home, she at last told George Butler, offering him a golden token of her constant affection, that she could bear these miseries no longer, and that they must separate.   He pleaded the impropriety of her conflict after such evidence that the appointment was divine.   His plea was the waste of words. She dismissed him utterly and forever.   This I had by the favor of George Butler himself.   Here Abner Blaisdell, Moses Butler, their families, their friends, and everybody else had another fair opportunity allowed them by Lydia Blaisdell herself, to search, examine, reflect, deliberate, and investigate the deception, if there was any.

A vessel was now in the river, bound to a port about 200 miles from this place, where lived some of her near kindred.[34]   Thither she was determined to go, and made preparation for the voyage, that if possible she might find repose on some distant shore. But the miraculous voice solemnly warned her, in the hearing of several witnesses, that her efforts were vain, and that her affliction would sail with her.

By the direction of the Specter given to one of those witnesses, the dismissed was recalled. Not long after, the nuptials were celebrated, and thus the Specter obtained one of those ends, which were only subordinate to other ends of far superior magnitude and importance.

These superior ends you will know hereafter, but they cannot — they must not be written.

# LETTER III
## *FURTHER EVIDENCE DEDUCED*
## *FROM THE APPEARANCES OF THE SPECTER*

My Dear Sir, In compliance with your request, I proceed in the argument that some persons among us have seen and conversed with the dead. Of the five corporal senses, only three are capable of information by events of this nature. These are seeing, feeling, and hearing. To all these three senses, evidence has been addressed in favor of the apparition in this place. I would now contemplate the evidence obtained by the senses of seeing and feeling.

The times, places, and modes of her appearing were various. Sometimes she appeared to be alone, as the events which followed for witness, for the testimony of events is sometime more valid than that of persons. Sometimes she appeared to two or three; then to five or six; then to ten or twelve; again to twenty, and once to more than forty witnesses. She appeared in several apartments of Abner Blaisdell's house, and several times in the cellar. She also appeared at other houses, and several times in the open field, as already observed.[35] There, white as the light, she moved like a cloud above the ground in personal form and magnitude, in the presence of more than forty people.[36] She tarried with them till after daylight, and vanished, not because she was afraid of the. sun, for she had then several times appeared when the sun was shining. Once in particular, when she appeared in the room where the family was about eleven o'clock in the day, they all left the house, but convinced of the impropriety of their conduct their conduct, they returned.[37]

At another time, when several neighbors were at the house, and were conversing on these remarkable events, a young lady in the company declared that, though she had heard a discourse of the Specter, she would never believe that there had been a Specter among us, unless she could see her.

In a few minutes after, the Specter appeared to several persons and said she must come in the room where the company was.[38] One of those who saw her pleaded that she would not. The Specter then asked, "Is there a person here who desires to see me." The young lady was then called, who, with several others saw the Specter. "Here I am," said she. "Satisfy yourselves." The lady owned she was satisfied. It was now about two o'clock in the day. In short the ghost appeared or conversed, or performed both almost as frequently in the day, as in the night. But will Christians argue that the appearance of an angel to the shepherds was a fiction because it happened in the night?[39]

In all the appearances of the Specter she was as white as the light, and this whiteness was as clear and visible in a dark cellar and dark night as when she appeared in the open field and in the open day. At a certain time, August 9-10, 1800, she informed a number of people that she meant to appear before them (for she frequently conversed without appearing at all) that they must stand in order and behave in a solemn manner: "For the Lord," said she, "is a God of order." Accordingly, she appeared and vanished before them several times. At first they saw a small body of light, which continually increased till it formed into the shape and magnitude of a person.

This personal shape approached so near to George Butler that he put his hand upon it and it passed down through the apparition as through a body of light, in the view of six or seven witnesses. There were now thirteen persons present, who all saw the apparition except two.[40] And five others, whether they were looking another way, or were prevented by some standing before them, or whatever might be the cause, did not see this attempt of handling the apparition.

50

But I attend to your reasoning. "If this extraordinary fact be true, like a pity it is that there were no more witnesses! Would not the evidence have been greater had it been acquired by all the eleven?" The more extraordinary the fact, the more numerous should be the witnesses. This is the opinion naturally entertained by mankind everywhere. Hence it follows that *all* of those eleven persons were not then practicing artifice, for then they would all have seen this extraordinary fact.

The five who did not see it, saw that which was very little short of it. They saw that which rose into personal form, face, and features in a moment, returned to a shapeless mass in a moment, resumed the person in a moment, and vanished again in a moment. They saw that which was not *afraid* to be handled by them, for she passed slowly by them near enough for that purpose.

The transfiguration of Christ was a very extraordinary fact. Out of all his twelve disciples, why chose he only three to be eyewitnesses of it?[41]

As to the six witnesses, not one of them has ever been accused or even suspected of being concerned in the supposed artifice.[42] Some of them are aged, others young. They had, and still have, professions, employments and interests widely different and belong to four different families. It is the fixed and settled opinion of our opponents here, that two of them are not only persons of integrity, but were ensnared by others through the whole scene.

These two persons soon after confirmed what they had now seen and experienced by solemn, practical, and most deliberate oaths in the presence of eighty people. For one of them made a prayer at the re-interment, expressing his belief of what he had seen, and the other solemnly declared to all the assembly, as soon as the prayer was finished, that this solemnity was ordered by the Specter, to be observed by his means. He also confirmed the same by an express verbal oath before the civil magistrate.

# LETTER IV
## *EVIDENCE PRODUCED BY THE DISCOURSE OF THE SPECTER*

Dear Sir, I would now present to your consideration the conversation of the Specter. But I shall first observe the objection urged against some part of it.

At the time when she appeared to several persons at two o'clock in the day, she said she must come into the room, where the company were, but was prevented by earnest entreaty.[43] This, they say, was a falsehood.

At another time when she walked in company with forty people, she went with them only to one house, though she had informed them that she must go to two houses.[44] She indeed went forward in order to visit the other house, but was again prevented by earnest entreaty. This was a fault like the other.

Observe a similar case in Gen. 19: 2-3. "And he said, behold now, my lords, turn in, I pray you, into your servant's house, and tarry all night and wash your feet, and ye shall rise up early and go on your ways, and they said, *nay, but we will abide in the street all night.* But he pressed upon them greatly, and *they turned in unto him and entered into his house.*"

Several credible persons say, "She promised nearly fifty people to convince them of her being such as she professed to be, if they would comply with a certain condition. They complied, and went off unconvinced." But credible persons are sometimes mistaken, and so, perhaps, they were now, because other persons, as credible and as numerous, who stood nearer to and had better advantage of understanding the voice, declare that it was not the Specter, but Abner Blaisdell, who said that the company, by complying, would be convinced. But he was mistaken. They went off, in general, unconvinced at that time. The Specter uttered but few words and withdrew. This was the night of August 9, 1800. In that company were the best of people, conducting in a sober manner, but others uttered such profanity and derision as rendered them unworthy to obtain conviction. On this account the Spirit afterwards declared that she could not manifest herself among them. Christ himself, in a certain place, could not do many mighty works because of their unbelief. It is easy enough to treat any affair with derision when we have not fully discovered what it is.[45]

A scorner seeketh wisdom and findeth it not.[46]

This company in general went off with the full persuasion that the whole affair was mere legerdemain, and that the few words of the Specter, which they had heard, were only the words of Lydia Blaisdell herself—though they had been expressly told by an unsuspected person, who held her by the hand when the words were uttered, that she did not speak, that the voice was at a distance from her. But they were moderns, and the witness was rejected, and, as it was plainly a different voice from that of Lydia Blaisdell, or any other that ever they had heard, necessity, the mother of invention, produced their hypothesis that Lydia Blaisdell had used some sounding instrument.

But several of the company still remained at the house. To them Lydia Blaisdell complained of the unjust reproach which encompassed her. "What have I done," said she, "that I must suffer all this?" "Nothing, dear, you have done nothing," answered a voice immediately in the vacant space of the room. Then about fourteen persons, by the direction of the Specter, went into the cellar. As soon as they were there, the Specter said to Lydia Blaisdell, "Go up and sit with others on the kitchen hearth,[47] that this company may know that it is not you who speaks." After she was gone up, the ghost conversed with the company on several topics suited to authenticate her mission.

She mentioned several incidents of her past life, known only to her husband, as he declared, and asked him if he remembered them. He said, "Yes." She asked him if he had told them. He answered, "No," and of such a nature were those incidents as to render it utterly improbable that he ever should have mentioned them before. This was at the time when he attempted to handle the apparition.[48]

It is objected against her that she told who was in heaven and who was in hell. She indeed mentioned the world of misery, as the eternal portion of the finally impenitent, but I find not the least evidence of her particularizing any person or persons as being in that miserable state.

She indeed mentioned several deceased persons as being in a state of happiness, and who can prove the impropriety of this, though indeed it is not what we should have expected?

Once when she conversed with about fourteen persons, Abner Blaisdell, having heard that his father was sick, asked the Specter whether she knew any thing or not, concerning him?[49] "Your father," she replied, "is in heaven, praising God with the angels." He afterwards found that his father, two hundred miles distant, died seven days before this answer of the ghost. True, the news might come from thence in that interval. But his friends at York, where his father lived, utterly deny that they sent the news in the course of these days. Suppose, however, the news did some way or other come. Could any deceiver, improving the circumstance, know what questions Abner Blaisdell would ask, so as to be sure they could all be answered? Or was Abner Blaisdell himself in the plot? "No," say our opponents, "his piety, his veracity, and his utter aversion to the purpose of it, forbid the suspicion." It is therefore *probable* that the same creature, who appeared and disappeared so often in the view of the people, and could tell them where they should be and what they would say and do in future time, was the true author of this information.

At a certain time, when thirty people were convened to hear her conversation, the name of a certain woman, who was absent, happened to be introduced. "That woman," said the ghost, "has enjoyed a revival lately."[50] Immediately, one of the company went to her and asked what had lately been the state of her mind. She related it to him, and he told her that her information and that of the Specter agreed. Upon this she came and saw the Specter, heard her conversation for several hours, and expressed abundant satisfaction and delight.

At the time when fifty people heard her discourse, while more that forty saw her, to some of them, who had no more believed these extraordinary events than mankind now do in general, she mentioned several occurrences of her past life known to them and her, but not divulged, in order to satisfy them that she was the very person she professed to be.[51] Almost all this company had been acquainted with her in her lifetime, and a considerable number of them very intimately. She desired that any of them would ask what questions they pleased, for the removal of any doubts respecting her, which might exist in their minds. Accordingly, certain persons did propose several questions respecting a number of events in her past life not divulged, which were so minute and circumstantial as to render the hypothesis of their being so exactly rehearsed, as now to become the medium of artifice, utterly absurd and irrational. To all these inquiries she gave complete, satisfactory answers.

But not to detain you, I will now only ask, *How shall I judge of these facts?* Shall I suppose that some artful girl personating that deceased woman could present herself before forty people well acquainted with that woman in her lifetime? Tell them by a voice inimitable not to be afraid—to stand as near as they pleased, and ask as many questions as they pleased—and all without fear of discovery? What subtle person would not be subtle enough to avoid such a perilous situation?

# LETTER V
## *THE EVIDENCE DEDUCED FROM HER PREDICTIONS*

Dear Sir, I must now ask your attention to the arguments furnished by her predictions.

She foretold what the opinion and conduct of mankind would be with regard to her, and the ill treatment which Abner Blaisdell's family would receive on her account. She not only declared the necessity, but foretold the certainty of the marriage, at an hour when both the parties and both their families opposed it, if there was anything to be known by the harmony of words and actions. Yet the attachment of the parties seems to have been mutual from first to last. The solution of the paradox is future: for mankind have more than one character, and the elector of Æsop will despise what a jeweler would prize.[52]

She not only predicted the prosecution, but named a particular person as one who would certainly be present at the court for a witness, eleven months before these events took place.[53]

She named another particular person, as one who should be present at the trial by the Grand Jury, and foretold what kind of language he would utter in their presence, eleven months before the accomplishment.

In about a month after, that is, ten months before the accomplishment, an oath of its existence was given before a magistrate. The person, too, who is the subject of this prediction, and fulfilled it, was never a friend, but invariably the foe of the Specter from first to last. She foretold to forty people the issue of that trial, eleven months before the accomplishment. To the genuine friends of literature in this place, who were sincerely opposing superstition and legerdemain, this prediction was made known.

They were warned of the disadvantage which they must suffer if they persisted.

They disbelieved the prediction, despised it, and became the involuntary subjects of its fulfillment at the time appointed. Within thirty hours after Lydia Blaisdell's marriage, the Specter predicted that she would become the parent of but one child and then die. Ten months after this her child was born, and she died the next day. The safe return of one bound to the West Indies was also foretold and accomplished.[54]

These predictions are all fulfilled and were previously and sufficiently known in this vicinity for evidence that they *were* such. She uttered several predictions now accomplished. But as these events might possibly be foreknown or strongly conjectured by other means, the mention of them is omitted. Not only her words, but her behavior too, manifested the spirit of prophecy. The re-interment of the child was a practical oath, and never would have been thought of but for her direction.[55] Friends and foes were all in one condition—all unable to conceive or even to conjecture the design of it, till it was manifested eighteen months afterwards, by certain, special, unexpected events of Divine Providence. If then we take an impartial and connecting view of these and all the preceding evidences, how absurd is the hypothesis that all these evidences could be, in effect, either of imagination or artifice! How much more rational is the opinion which has obtained credit in all ages and nations, that the spirit of deceased persons do sometimes appear, however incapable we are of learning all the purposes for which such events are designed!

By misapprehension and misinformation, piety and veracity may give you an account very different from mine. But ask those people of piety and veracity who were present when the greatest of these events took place. I tell you they will not deny these facts.

# LETTER VI
## *MISCELLANY*

If the preceding arguments can be received, perhaps you will not indulge distrust if I subjoin something of my own experience, confirmed by two other persons who saw the apparition in the same field in the same half hour.

Sometime in July, 1806, in the evening, I was informed by two persons that they had just seen the Specter in the field.[56]

About ten minutes after, I went out, not to see a miracle, for I believed that they had been mistaken. Looking toward an eminence, twelve rods distance from the house, I saw there, as I supposed, one of the white rocks. This confirmed my opinion on their Specter, and I paid no more attention to it. Three minutes after, I accidentally looked in the same direction, and the white rock was in the air, its form a complete globe, white with a tincture of red, like the damask rose, and its diameter about two feet.

Fully satisfied that this was nothing ordinary, I went toward it for more accurate examination.

While my eye was constantly upon it, I went on four or five steps, when it came to me from the distance of eleven rods, as quick as lightning, and instantly assumed a personal form with a female dress, but did not appear taller than a girl seven years old. While I looked upon her, I said in my mind, "You are not tall enough for the woman who has so frequently appeared among us." Immediately, she grew up as large and as tall as I considered that woman to be. Now she appeared glorious. On her head was the representation of the sun diffusing the luminous, rectilinear rays everyway to the ground. Through the rays I saw the personal form, and the woman's dress. Then I recollected the objection of the *Encyclopedia*, that, "Ghosts always appear to one alone." Now, said my mind, I see you as plainly as ever I saw a person on earth, but were I to converse with you an hour, what proof could I produce that I ever conversed with you at all? This, with my fear, was the reason why I did not speak to her. But my fear was connected with ineffable pleasure.

Life, simplicity, purity, glory, all harmonizing in this celestial form, had the most delightful effect on my mind. And they are appeared such a dullness afterwards upon all corporal objects as I never perceived before. I went into the house and gave the information, not doubting that she had come to spend some time with us, as she had before. We went out to see her again, but to my great disappointment, she had vanished. Then I saw one of the great errors of my life. That I had not spoken to her has been the matter of my regret from that hour to this. My word without witness has not been tedious. Believed or rejected, it may do you no harm.

On the more sure ground of attestation, I will now relate some instances of her appearing or conversing, or performing both, in the daytime.

Sometime in March, 1800, she talked a few minutes without appearing, at eight o'clock in the morning, and promised to come again that day. At two o'clock, performed her promise, and talked with four people two hours. It was then she uttered these words: "Though my body is consumed, and all turned to dust, my soul is as much alive, as before I left the body."

This conversation was indeed in the cellar, but the place was enlightened by her radiance.

May 21, at ten o'clock, she appeared to two persons, and sent a message to another.

May 25, 10 o'clock. Appeared and conversed with two witnesses, while a third person only heard the conversation, and revealed that by which the same was proved to others.

May 26. She appeared at eight o'clock in the morning, and talked with four persons an hour and a half. In half an hour after, she appeared and talked with the same four persons, while two others only heard a voice without knowing what was said.

May 27. Talked with two persons, and promised to be present at a meeting of about twenty people, which was to be held the next day in the evening.[57] Accordingly, she appeared at this meeting to two other persons who were ignorant of the promise. The assembly was immediately interrupted by the declaration that "The Spirit is come." None, however, could distinctly see her, but those two persons. The next evening after, she conversed with a third couple of persons in company with the first two, mentioned her promise as being fulfilled, and told them by her inimitable voice to whom she had appeared. As a further confirmation that she had been really present on this occasion, she did about two months afterwards talk several hours in the midst of the assembly of forty-eight people, while she was visible to two, and only two, of that number.[58] These two people were a fourth couple distinct from the other six. Such is the testimony of these eight persons.

Her conversation was always with grace, seasoned with salt, very affecting and delightful.

August 13, at 10 o'clock, she talked with three persons invisibly. At two o'clock the same day, she appeared and talked to three people in the hearing of five other persons.[59]

Thus have you received a general, but very imperfect, account of these extraordinary events.

And now because a juggler will appear to check a musket ball with the point of his knife, form animals, and perform a thousand other idle wonders, will any lover of truth indulge the inference that all the preceding phenomena are of the same nature? Do these magicians reveal and establish truths, the knowledge of which is of great importance to certain persons now, and a public utility hereafter?  No, their miracles are without meaning, and their design is pecuniary profit, or else to show what they can do to gratify the vain curiosity of spectators.

Mountebanks do not *commonly* unite their employment with religious order, prayer, and praise, or with solemn admonitions of life and death, blessing and cursing.  Nor do their idle exhibitions so harmonize with the common operations of Divine Providence as that the former and the latter have manifestly the same ultimate purposes.  This harmony is more than artifice can produce.  Besides, who ever knew an instance like this in view, which, with all its circumstances, was afterwards fairly proved to be a deception?  And if mountebanks never did exhibit such a variety in such circumstances, without the least partial discovery, we may be sure they never could.  For doubtless they have done all they could do to impose on mankind by this species of inequity.

It would perhaps afford you some satisfaction to know what other persons here would say respecting these transactions.  I shall therefore improve the first opportunity to send you a copy of the oaths and attestations, which have been given by those who favor the cause, and by those who oppose it.

I continued yours to serve for the promotion of truth.

−Abraham Cummings

***

# TESTIMONY BY EYE-WITNESSES

***

Abraham Cummings, a writer and traveling evangelist, collected 31 eye-witness testimonies and formal depositions on the Nelly Butler hauntings and included them with his letters in his 1826 publication *Immortality Proved by the Testimony of Sense: in Which Is Considered the Doctrine of Spectres, and the Existence of a Particular Spectre.* Internal references indicate that witnesses submitted their personal accounts soon after the climax of the hauntings on August 13-14, 1800, but also before the re-interment of Nelly Butler's child, which probably took place in the fall of that year.

Of the testimony he collected, Cummings had the following to say: "With all these witnesses I am intimately acquainted. I took these testimonies from their lips, for the most part, separately. I wrote them, read them in their hearing, and obtained their approbation of what I had written. I made but little alteration in their language."[1] While Cummings strove to be impartial, he nonetheless heavily edited the accounts, and no record exists of the originals he had transcribed by hand. He writes, "The following pages, for brevity's sake, present only the extracts from some of the oaths and numerous testimonies of those who oppose and of those who favor the cause."[2] Nevertheless, no other paranormal event in Early America involved so much careful documentation.

# DEPOSITIONS

### DEPOSITION OF CAPTAIN PAUL SIMPSON[3]

About the first of August, 1800, David Hooper and his wife came to my house and desired me to go to Abner Blaisdell's with them. After we got there, they said the Spirit sent for me.

I went down into the cellar, and soon after it rapped. I asked what it wanted. It told me that I had done wrong; I had become hard against her — that I had disbelieved. I told her I had. She said that Satan had tempted me and that I had sinned. I asked her if she loved Christ. She said, "Yes, I do." I told her the work of the saints was to praise God. "Yes," she said, "and Christ too," and broke out in singing alleluias.

At another time she ordered us to place ourselves two and two, and she would follow us to Captain James Miller's, and ordered us to sing a psalm as we went. In going there I never saw her. As we walked back, I walked behind. I looked back and saw her. She appeared to me dressed all in white, as bright a white as ever I saw, and had the appearance of a woman and bigness. –Paul Simpson

### THE DEPOSITION OF MRS. SARAH SIMPSON

On August 7, Abner Blaisdell came to my house and said the voice had sent him for more witnesses, and that Samuel Simpson and I must go to his house. I was very much affrighted, and could not think what he wanted. He said the Spirit had sent him for more witnesses, and that I must go. I then told him that Samuel Simpson said the apparition had appeared at our house the night before. My husband and I then went with him. After we had been there some time, there was a knocking — some spoke to her. She then asked if we wanted to know who she was. It was answered, "Yes." She then said three times, "I was once Nelly Butler." There were many questions asked, which she answered very directly. I asked,

"Are you from happiness or misery?" To which she answered, "I am from above, and am come on God's message," and fell to singing alleluias.

After discoursing some time, she said she was going to appear to us, and we must place ourselves two and two and come into the cellar, and she would show herself. We complied. I was of the last couple who went into the cellar. It was my desire not to see her. She said those who did not desire to see her should not. I saw nothing. And though she was so near to me, as I was told by Paul Blaisdell, as that I could touch her if I had put out my hand, and I looked to see her, yet, as I had said I did not want to see her, I could not see her. I also, while in the field, looked to see her, yet I did not see her. – Sarah Simpson

### THE DEPOSITION OF MR. THOMAS URANN[4]

In August 3, 1800, I was at the house of Abner Blaisdell.[5] I went on purpose to hear and see what I could concerning a Spirit which was said to be there. In the evening there was a knocking round the house, but nothing spoke. We all concluded there would be nothing said or seen. The next morning about daybreak there seemed to be knockings round the house, and in the chamber, and round my bed. We immediately got up, and going down I took a candle, lighted it, and went into the cellar alone, examining if there was no one there to deceive us. I could not see anybody. I came back. Abner Blaisdell, with all in the house, went down cellar — we heard a knocking. Someone spoke in the name of God, and asked what she wanted. She asked if we wanted to know who she was. We answered, "Yes." She told us she was once Nelly Butler. She then said to me, "You have often said that I am a devil or a witch." I then asked her if she was from the God of heaven or from misery. She answered, "I am from above, praising God and the Lamb." She then broke out in praise. She then told us that she had come to warn us from sin, and that if there was not a change before the soul left the body, we should be forever miserable. She then told us the danger a sinner was in, out of Christ, and told us that she should rise in the Day of Judgment against us. I told her I had a great desire that she should appear. And then she appeared to us all who had a desire to see her.

She appeared like a person who was wrapped in a white sheet, appearing and disappearing several times. It was near sunrise at this time.

She then told us that was the day that Christ rose from the dead, and that it was God's precious time, and must be kept unto him.

Lydia Blaisdell was not in the cellar while the foregoing talk was. The Spirit asked me if I would not clear Lydia. I answered I would, for it was not she who talked.
–Thomas Urann

### DEPOSITION OF CAPTAIN GEORGE BUTLER

When I was called to talk with this voice, I asked, "Who are you?" [6] It answered, "I was once your wife." The voice asked me, "Do you not remember what I told you when I was alive?" I answered, "I do not really know what you mean." The voice said, "Do you not remember I told you I did not think I should live long with you? I told you that, if you were to leave me, I should never wish to change my condition, but that if I was to leave you, I could not blame you if you did."

This passed between me and my first wife, while she was alive, and there was no living person within hearing, but she and myself, and I am sure that this was never revealed to any person, and no living person could have told it to me before the voice did. As Lydia Blaisdell and I stood side and side alone,[7] she had her left arm round me and her right hand hold of the forward part of my waistcoat, her head leaning against my breast. There was something appeared to my view right before me, like a person in a winding sheet and her arms folded

69

under the winding sheet, and on her arm there appeared to be a very small child. By this appearance I did not know possibly but I might be deceived. I reached out my left hand to take hold of it. I saw my hand in the middle of it, but could feel nothing. The same evening it appeared and disappeared to me three times. –George Butler

HANCOCK, SS—SULLIVAN, *August 1800.* [8] *Personally appeared Paul Simpson, Sarah Simpson, Thomas Urann, and George Butler, who, being carefully examined as to the truth of the above declarations, made solemn oaths that the statements were true.*

# TESTIMONIES

EDITOR'S NOTE: *Abraham Cummings, who collected the following eye-witness accounts, organized them into two categories. "The testimonies by difference of opinion have naturally two parts," he writes, "that of the opponents and that of the adherents. The first part presents the attestation of those who consider these phenomena as a scene of wickedness."*[9]

## TESTIMONY FROM OPPONENTS

### *TESTIMONY OF MISS HANNAH GATCOMB*

August 9-10. I was at the house of Abner Blaisdell, by the persuasion of others. For as to myself I made very light of the matter, supposing that the whole was the contrivance of certain persons, and I believe still that nothing good appeared there.

We heard rappings, and these sounds were spoken to, but no answer obtained. After much altercation (which is needless to rehearse) we all came out of the cellar, and all went off, except a few persons, of whom I was one. Some of Abner Blaisdell's family uttered severe expressions against those who went off and did not believe. "What do you want they should believe," said I. "For my part I see nothing to believe." Immediately, Lydia Blaisdell came in from the entry very much affrighted. "If anyone desires to be convinced," said she, "let him look there in the entry." I looked there and saw nothing. Soon after this, while Lydia Blaisdell was sitting on the foot of a bed, we heard a sound right against her on the outside of the house. George Butler told her to speak to it. At first she refused. They told her she must. Then she said to it, "If I am guilty stay away; if I am clear, in the name of the Lord clear me." The Spirit then rapped very hard, so as to shake the house. Some of the company said she must go into the cellar. "So I must," said she. "If I do not, she will come into the room, and if she does, I shall die.[10] Who will go with me?" Dorcas Abbott said she would go. They went,[11] and soon after we all went down. Then I plainly heard the voice say to Lydia Blaisdell, "Go up, that the people may not think it is you who speaks." I saw her go up into the room, and heard at the same time the voice in the cellar. Abner Blaisdell asked the Spirit whence she came. She answered, "I am from heaven. I am with God and with Christ— angels and seraphim, praising God. Glory, glory, glory." Abner Blaisdell asked why she did not manifest herself in the forepart of that night to all the people. She answered, "I was not permitted to come where there was so much sin." The Spirit then said to Abner Blaisdell, "Ask the people if they are convinced." He did so, and I among the rest answered that I was. But I think otherwise now. God knew who would be there the forepart of that night. Why did he send her? Then the Spirit said, "I must appear," and by her direction we placed ourselves in order. Then I saw a white appearance, at first not more than a foot in height, but it appeared larger and larger, and more plainly, and when it came nearer to me, I was struck with fear and left the cellar, but others told me that afterwards they saw the Spirit plainly.

August 13-14, I again went to Abner Blaisdell's with forty-seven persons. The Spirit now told us again that she was from heaven, and that she was once Nelly Hooper. After much conversation the Spirit said that some of the people were faint, and could not hear all that was to be said, and that we must go up and refresh ourselves. "You must go with me to two places this night," said she, "and you must be ready at one o'clock." "What o'clock is it now?" said Abner Blaisdell. She said, "Twelve, twelve, twelve." We went up immediately and looked on the watch, and it was exactly twelve. In a short time, hearing the usual sign, we returned. Among many other words which I do not remember, Richard Downing asked the Spirit if she knew him. She answered, "Yes," and called him by name. He asked if she was ever at his house. She answered that she had been once there with her mother. At length she told us that we must go up, and she would walk with us behind, with Lydia Blaisdell. "But you must walk in order, two and two," said she, "singing a psalm, for God is a God of order." Some person asked when she would be ready. She said, "I will let you know." Some person again asked what o'clock it was. She answered, *"One."* We went up and again looked on the watch, and it was *one*. We attended prayer, and immediately after she knocked. A psalm was chosen, which the greatest number of us could best remember, and it was sung as we walked. I was now far forward and did not see the Spirit. When we came to James Miller's, the Spirit rapped there, and James Miller with Paul Blaisdell and some others went into the cellar, and I heard them talk, but could not understand what was said to them.

Then word came to us that we must stand out in the field before the house — that she would appear before us, and walk with Lydia Blaisdell, that the people might be convinced that Lydia Blaisdell had told the truth in relating that she had walked with her before. Then we all stood before the house. Lydia Blaisdell put on a black cloak, and when she had walked a little distance from us, as before directed by the Spirit, I heard her groan bitterly, and soon after I saw the appearance of a woman in white, walking with her. Suddenly, Lydia Blaisdell sung a part of that hymn called "New Jerusalem."[12] Then she came to us, and we all went back in order to Abner Blaisdell's. I then looked back and saw a person in white walking with Lydia Blaisdell. After we returned to the house, Lydia Blaisdell appeared very weary and exhausted. I asked her at what time the Spirit came to her. She told me it was after she had walked a little distance from the people. "When you heard me groan," said she, "then I saw it coming toward me. I am always more afraid when I only see it, than I am after it has spoken to me.[13] And she now told me not to be scared, that she was not come to hurt me, and that if I would sing a hymn, it would expel my fears." –Hannah Gatcomb


### TESTIMONY OF MR. PAUL SIMPSON, JR.

August 9, 1800. I was at Abner Blaisdell's, with many more, and heard the sound of knocking. It was addressed, and a voice answered, but I could not understand it. Several persons spoke, but received no satisfactory answer. The people generally concluded that the whole affair was some deception. Therefore, they went off and I among them. But my reflections on that singular knocking induced me to say to two young men, "If you will go back, I will, and find out something more, if possible. For I am no more satisfied now, than I was before I went to that house." We went back. Abner Blaisdell asked us why we returned. I told him that we had all gone off with the opinion that the whole affair was a scheme contrived by his daughters, and nothing more, and I meant if possible to find them out. "You must think as you please," said he. "I am clear, and I believe my family is." I told him I wished to see all his family sitting in one part of the room. They complied. Then I took a candle and stood in the midst of the room. After several minutes, something rapped near where two of us stood, and from thence removed to several parts of the house. "What do you think of it?" said Abner Blaisdell? "It appears," said I, "to be strange." "We will go into the cellar," said Abner Blaisdell, "and, if you think anybody is there, search the cellar through with a candle." We did so. I came out last and was careful and watched, so that I was sure that no person went down. Also the outer door was fast. Then again we heard the sound of knocking. It was addressed, and conversation followed, in the midst of which Abner Blaisdell said to me, "If you think any living person talks, go forward and grasp that person." I went forward a few steps, but was so convinced that

74

nobody was there, that I consider all further attempts as useless.

After much discourse, which I cannot remember, the Spirit told us that we must go up and come down again in order, two and two, and she would appear to us. We did so, and I saw the apparition at first about two feet in height, but as it drew nearer to me, it appeared as tall as a person. I saw this appearance passing *close by me and from me five or six times*. At last it diminished to about a foot in height and then vanished.

–Paul Simpson, Jr.


### TESTIMONY OF MISS SALLY MARTIN

August 13, 1800, I was at Abner Blaisdell's house, with more than forty people, besides their own family, and heard knockings. We all wondered when we heard a sound on one side or corner of the house, the next sound on the opposite side or corner, and a third sound equally distant from the second, and so on for a number of sounds, while the succession was as rapid as one sound could be clearly distinguished from another. We were sure that no person, nor even several persons, could make sounds so distant from each other in such quick succession, even were it possible for them to be in or near the places of these sounds, without discovery. By that desire of the Spirit and Abner Blaisdell, we went into the cellar. Abner Blaisdell told the people to stand back and give the Spirit room, and not crowd so near her. "Don't crowd her," said he. "She cannot talk if you crowd her."

When we were placed, Abner Blaisdell ordered the candle to be blown out and stood before the company next to the Spirit.[14] When these things were done, the affair was become as dark to me as the cellar was. I heard much conversation with several people by a voice which I never heard before. This voice at last told us to go up and go to a certain house and she would go with us. We did as the voice told us, and, as we went, I saw a personal form, as white as anything could possibly appear, walking by Lydia Blaisdell's side, with locked arms. When we came to the only outer door of the house, I saw this form at a distance from me, abroad, though near the house. I went in and heard a knocking immediately under the floor. In two or three minutes I heard the same voice that I had heard before, talking with James Miller.

By the desire of the voice, we stood before the house that she might appear to us. There I saw the personal form as plainly as ever I saw a living person, and I saw the same form vanish before me in a moment.  –Sally Martin


### TESTIMONY OF CAPTAIN JAMES MILLER

August 7.  Abner Blaisdell came to my house and desired me to go to his own, where I might hear and see for myself.  He also went to Captain Samuel Simpson's with the same request.  Captain Simpson and his wife, S—B—, and N—G—, who were there, came with him to my house, and we all went to Abner Blaisdell's.  When we had been there some minutes, Samuel Simpson, by desire, prayed.  His prayer was immediately followed by a knocking, and we all went into the cellar. Abner Blaisdell asked what was wanted, and who it was. It answered, "I was once Nelly Hooper."[15]  I asked, "How was man made?"  "Out of the dust," said the voice. "Dust thou art, and unto dust thou shalt return. You have the Bible, and that is God's truth, and do you abide by it.  Love God, and keep his commandments."    After some conversation with Sarah Simpson and others, she said, "I must go," and we heard no more.  It was now abroad daylight, the outer cellar door being open, and utterly impossible that any living person should be there, but those whom we could see and know. The voice was about six feet from me.

August 9. I went to that house with many people, among whom I observed much disorderly behavior. The Spirit spoke but little, and I returned with a resolution to go no more to that house on such an errand.

August 14. Just before daylight, I heard singing, as I lay in bed, approaching to my house. Presently, by my leave, my house was filled with people, and I heard knockings on the floor. By the desire of certain persons, I went into the cellar with Paul Blaisdell. After some discourse of the voice with him, which I understood not, I heard sounds of knocking near me. I asked, "What do you want of me?" It answered, "I have come to let you know that I can speak in this cellar as well as in the other.[16] Are you convinced?" I answered, "I am." "Now," said the voice, "the company must be solemn and stand in order before your door—I am going to appear. Now do you remember that I was once Nelly Hooper?" We went up and complied with her direction, and I saw a personal shape coming toward us, white as the light. By the Specter's order, as I was informed, Lydia Blaisdell went toward her. "Lydia," said the Specter, "you are scared. You must sing." Then she sung a hymn. The Spirit came almost to us, then turned, and Lydia Blaisdell with her, and went several rods towards Samuel Simpson's and appeared to take her by the hand to urge her on further, and disappeared in our sight.

Lydia Blaisdell returned and informed the company, as I was told, that if they would walk to Abner Blaisdell's solemnly as to a funeral, the Spirit would walk with Lydia Blaisdell behind them. The company did so. But I being far forward, saw nothing. Lydia Blaisdell had expressed her unwillingness to go to Samuel Simpson's, and was excused, as she afterwards told us. –James Miller

## TESTIMONY OF MRS. MARY GORDON

On the 3rd of August, 1800, about two hours before daylight, while I slept in Abner Blaisdell's house, I was waked by the sound of knocking.[17] I got up, and with about twenty others went into the cellar. There I heard such a voice speaking to us as I never heard before nor since. It was shrill, but very mild and pleasant.

Abner Blaisdell, in addressing the voice, said that several persons (of whom I was one) had come from a distance to obtain satisfaction, and desired that she would tell us who she was, and the design of her coming. She answered, "I was once Nelly Hooper, and after I was married, I was Nelly Butler." After much conversation upon the design of her coming, she appeared to us. At first the apparition was a mere mass of light, then grew into personal form, about as tall as myself. We stood in two ranks about four or five feet apart. Between these ranks she slowly passed and re-passed, so that any of us could have handled her. When she passed by me, her nearness was that of contact, so that, if there had been a substance, I should have certainly felt it. The glow of the apparition had a constant tremulous motion. At last the personal form became shapeless — expanded everyway, and then vanished in a moment.

Then I examined my own white gown and handkerchief, but I could no more see them than if they had been black.

Nothing more being now seen or heard, we were moving to go up, when the voice spoke again and desired us to tarry longer. We did so, and the Spirit talked with us another hour, even till broad daylight. She mentioned to us the ill treatment which Abner Blaisdell's family had suffered by reproach and false accusation, and told us that they would, on her account, be more despised and ridiculed in time to come, than they had been already.

Her discourse concluded by a solemn exhortation to the old, the middle aged, and the young. The present life, she said, was but a moment, in which we must be renewed or be miserable forever.

In her address to the youth she observed that it was now the Lord's Day, and that we must retire to our homes, read the Bible, pray and keep the day holy. It was then she uttered these lines of Isaac Watts:

> This is the day when Christ arose
> So early from the dead;
> Why should I keep my eyelids closed,
> And waste my hours in bed?[18]

After speaking much more which I cannot remember, she sang praises and left us.

Her notes were very pleasant. Her words were in no higher style than common, yet were they exceedingly impressive.   –Mary Gordon


### TESTIMONY OF MRS. SALLY WENTWORTH

On the 2nd of January 1800, Hannah Blaisdell came to George Butler's house and informed me that the extraordinary voice which they had heard had declared itself to be that of my sister, and that I must go to her father's house.

I told her to her face that I did not believe it.

The next day I received the same message by three other persons, two of which belonged to two other families, and returned the same answer.   Nevertheless, to give satisfaction, George Butler, Moses Wentworth, and I went with them to that house.  George Butler and I examined the cellar with a candle, and in a few minutes after, Lydia and I went down there.  Paul Simpson and some others went with us, but none of them stood before us.  While I held Lydia by the arm, we heard the sound of knocking.  Lydia spoke, and a voice answered, the sound of which brought fresh to my mind that of my sister's voice, in an instant, but I could not understand it at all though it was within the compass of my embrace, and, had it

79

been a creature which breathed, it would have breathed in my face, and I had no impediment of hearing. But Lydia told me that it said, "We must live in peace and be united." Then we came up. But Paul Simpson with Lydia and others went down again. I passed through the room which led to the cellar into another room, and there I was much surprised when I plainly understood by the same kind of voice, still speaking in the cellar, these words, "I am the voice of one crying in the wilderness," and other sentences, which I cannot remember. This is testified by several others who were with me.[19]

From this time I cleared Lydia as to the voice, and accused the devil.

August 8, I was there again with about thirty others, and heard much conversation. Her voice was still hoarse and thick, like that of my sister on her deathbed,[20] but more hollow. Sometimes it was clear, and always pleasant. A certain person did, in my opinion very unwisely, ask her whether I was a true Christian. The reply was, "She thinks she is. She thinks she is. She is my sister."

August 13—14, I heard the same voice in the same place and did then believe it was that of my sister. She talked much with Paul Simpson and exhorted the people. James Springer asked her if I believed that she was my sister. The answer was, "She believes now." By the direction of the Spirit we went to James Miller's, but I never saw her.

Before I reached home that morning, the whole affair to me appeared a delusion, for she had said that she must go to two houses and went to but one. My real sister, I trust, is incapable of falsehood. Her countenance expressive of heavenly peace consoled me in her last hours.

Sometime after this, George Butler brought to me, from the Specter, the private conversation which I know I had with my sister in her lifetime, at a certain hour, when we were alone together, and which he declares he never knew before, as a token that I was her sister. It is true I had never revealed it to any person, and I do not believe that my sister ever did, but could not some evil spirit hear that conversation, and afterwards personate my sister, and reveal it to George Butler? For what purpose should my sister become visible to us? There was certainly no dispute nor difficulty in my father's family or that of George Butler's, which could be any reason for her coming.  –Sally Wentworth

### TESTIMONY OF MR. JEREMIAH BUNKER

On August 9, 1800, I went to Abner Blaisdell's, where there were about twelve people.

After hearing the discourse of the Specter, she appeared before us and disappeared several times.  She came close by me and three or four others several times, so that each of us could have handled her.  The personal shape, when it disappeared, first changed to a substance, without form, and then vanished in a moment where it was, and after a short space, the full personal form appeared again in a moment.  These changes I observed several times.  I thought then and ever since that the whole was a deception.  For I cannot see how there could be such a clear personal shape, where no living person was.  She was in the shape of a person as much as any person could be.
–Jeremiah Bunker

# TESTIMONY FROM ADHERENTS

NOTE BY ABRAHAM CUMMINGS: *The second part presents the attestation of those who favor the cause, or at least have not appeared openly against it. I have discoursed with all these persons, except two or three, whose names are mentioned in this testimony, and that they all attest to almost all the facts which are here related, as being known to them.*

### *TESTIMONY OF MR. ABNER BLAISDELL*

May 29, 1800. The Specter conversed with three of my family. To dispel their fears, she introduced her conversation by these words: "I have come again.[21] Be not afraid. I will not hurt you. I did not come here to hurt you. I am a friend to you all." One of them answered, "I cannot help being afraid." "You need not be," said the Specter. "You need not be. I never did hurt you, did I?" "No," it was answered. "And I shall not hurt you," said the Specter. "Put your things in place.[22] Conduct as formerly, for nothing will hurt you."

To George Butler the Specter said, "Be kind to your wife, for she will not be with you long. She will have but one child and then die." It was now that the Spirit sent a token to Joanna Hooper, her mother, by which Joanna Hooper declares she must have been her daughter.

On August 3, she discoursed with about twenty persons, of whom I was one.[23] "I come," said she, "to warn you against sin, and if there is not a change before the soul leaves the body, you will be forever miserable."

After the Spirit had spoken many things of this nature, Thomas Urann expressed his desire to see her. "You shall see me," said she. "I will appear to you all." She appeared and disappeared before us several times and talked while she appeared. She came close to us, and some said they saw the child in her arms. My son Paul observed it and said, "Her child is now in her arms." "So it is," said she. "So it is."

When it was daylight, she told us that this was the day when Christ rose from the dead—that it was God's precious time and must be kept holy, and that she must return to carry on the work of praise, and then sang praises and left us.

August 6. I had for some time heard that my father was sick, but had since received no news from him. I ventured to ask how my father did. "He is in heaven," said she, "praising God with the angels." I afterwards found by other means that my father died seven days before this. He lived two hundred miles from me.

When she left us at this time, the voice sounded in the air further and further from us, uttering these words: "I am in heaven, praising God and the Lamb with angels, archangels, cherubim, and seraphim. Glory, glory, glory to God and the Lamb. I am going. I am going. I am going to Christ."

August 8. About thirty people came to my house. That night the Specter had much solemn conversation with them on religious subjects. Mr. N. H——n expressed his desire to handle her, and she gave him liberty. Sometimes the inimitable voice would sound ten or twelve feet from us, then close to our face, then again at a distance, and these changes were instantaneous. After broad daylight, the outer door being open, when we could plainly see each other, the voice spoke to all, and said, "Let anyone who pleases come and handle me, for Christ says that a spirit hath not flesh and bones."

Some person then said to Mr. H——n, "Now if you want to handle her, why don't you go?"

Then he crowded through the people to the place where the voice was still speaking, and said, "I find nothing here to handle."

August 9, 1800. We placed ourselves in order, according to the direction of the Specter, and a white appearance, at first very small, rose before me and grew to a personal stature and form. It stood directly before George Butler, while he and Lydia Blaisdell stood beside each other.[24] I saw him put his hand on the apparition, and I saw his hand pass through it. Then it vanished. There were now about twelve persons here.

August 13, while I was at work in my field, I was told that the Spirit had sent for me.[25] I went into my house, heard a voice, but saw nothing.

This voice, which declared itself to be Nelly Hooper, said, "Call for my parents, P.S.S.C.,[26] his wife, and others who appear to you to know Christ, that they may hear and see, for they will tell the truth." I performed the errand, and those persons came with more than forty others that night. I went into the cellar and asked who should come. "They must all come," said she. "Leave not a soul behind." I gave the information, and they complied. The Spirit first asked her parents whether they believed she was her daughter, and they said, "Yes." "Do you want to see me?" said she. And they said, "No." She asked her father if he was ready to go with her, if the Lord should call him. "I am afraid I am not," said he, "but the Lord can make me willing." "That is right," she answered. Then after conversing with her mother, in a very affecting manner, she said to both, "You were my dear parents once, but now you are no more to me than others." Then to Paul Simpson she said, "You have become hard against me." "So I have," said he. "Do you love Christ?" "Yes, I do," said she. "Yes, I do." P.S. "Then you love me?" "Yes, I do. Do you not remember that soon after I was married, you told me that I was married to George Butler and how happy I should be, if I was married to Christ, and I said I was not, but I wished I was?" P.S. "Yes, I remember it very well." "Now I am married to Christ," said she. "Now I am married to Christ. Now I am married to Christ."

"You used to meet with us at my house, and once, at the time of a certain prayer, I observed you to be much affected."

"Yes, I was," said she," and the Lord was then breaking my heart."

I then spoke to her myself and said, "I never knew that you experienced a change of nature before you died, and I should be glad if you would tell when you experienced it." "It was," said she, "when I lay upon my deathbed." Then she spoke to her parents and reminded them of the conversation which had passed between them at that time, respecting the loss of her child. "Then it was," said she, "that I received my change."

After much other conversation, which I do not remember, the Spirit said to us, "There is one of this family who is not here."[27] Some person asked if we should go and call him. She said, "No, I am going where he is. They say I can appear nowhere but here, but I mean to convince them that I can appear in other places. I must appear before you all this night and go to the next house and to another. You must all go up and be ready to walk with me. But you must walk in order, two and two, solemnly, as if you were following a friend to the grave. For the Lord is a God of peace and not of confusion. Sing a psalm as you walk, and I will walk with Lydia after you." We all went up, and in about an hour after, we heard the token, and placed ourselves before the door, and hearing it again, we walked on to James Miller's, and the Spirit knocked under his floor. He and my son went down and, after conversing with my son, she told James Miller who she was, and the purpose of her coming to his house, and asked him if he was satisfied, and he told her that he was. Then she directed him to go up and tell the people to stand in order before the door, and she would appear before them in the field. They did so, and she appeared to them and disappeared, as some of them informed me. By her direction we walked back to my house in the same order, and then I saw her plainly about thirty feet from me, in the form and stature of a person, white as the light and moving after us like a cloud, without ambulatory motion.    –Abner Blaisdell

### TESTIMONY OF MISS MARY CARD

I am not only a witness to many things in the preceding relation, but I further declare that, on August 13, about two o'clock in the day, while Abner Blaisdell was gone for evidence, the Spirit knocked, and Margaret Miller and I went near to the place of the sound and asked what was wanted.

The Spirit answered, "I have come. I have come. Make room, for I am coming among you."[28] I pleaded that she would not. "I must. I must," said she. "Don't be scared." I answered we were poor sinful creatures and could not help it, and again earnestly entreated her not to come.

I now plainly saw her appear in shining white, and she asked me if any person in the house wanted to see her. I then called on Miss P.C., who in the same hour had said that, though she had heard the voice speak, she would not believe it was that of a ghost. I asked her now to come and see her, and she did. "Now," said the ghost, "satisfy yourselves. Here I am. Here I am. Satisfy yourselves." Miss P.C. answered that she was satisfied.[29] The ghost then spoke several other things which I cannot remember. −Mary Card


### TESTIMONY OF MISS MARGARET MILLER

I was present at the same time, and heard all that is here declared by Mary Card. I saw the apparition and heard her speak at the same time. −Margaret Miller


### TESTIMONY OF CAPTAIN PAUL SIMPSON[30]

January 3, 1800, I was at the house of Abner Blaisdell. His son Paul desired me to go with him into the cellar. I went down with him and his two sisters, and Mrs. C. M.

I heard a rapping and asked in the name of Christ what it wanted. I heard a voice considerably loud but could not understand it. But some who were present told me that it said: "I am the voice of one crying in the wilderness. Prepare ye the way of the Lord. Make his paths strait. Seek ye the Lord, while he may be found. Call upon him while he is near."[31]

After some silence it rapped again. I spoke to it in the name of Christ, and said, if there was anything it could utter for peace, to utter it. It answered, "I am not to be trifled with. I am not to be trifled with. I am not to be trifled with. Peace, peace, peace."[32]

Then they all went up, except Lydia and myself, and I held her by the hand. She was much terrified and said, "I feel so I cannot stay. I must go up." "Stay awhile," said I. "Perhaps it will speak again." "I cannot," said she, and began to urge me away. I consented, and when we had come up, she told me what I had myself perceived, that the cellar began to grow light, where the voice was uttered and that she heard a rushing noise.

Sometime after, I was in the same cellar with a number of people and heard a plain voice, clearly understood by others, but not at all by myself, though as near to it as others and free from deafness. The voice appeared to me inimitable.

August 8, I was there again with thirty others and heard the conversation of the Specter with several persons. Mr. N. H. mentioned his desire to handle her. "Handle me and see," said she, "for Christ tells you that a spirit is not flesh and bones."

Thomas Urann said, "If are a happy soul, intercede for me." The reply was, "None but Christ intercedes." "There are among us," said Thomas Urann, "several denominations of Christians: Presbyterians, Congregationalists, Baptists, and Methodists. Which of all these are right?" The voice answered, "There are good and bad of all sorts for the elect's sake."[33]

In August 13-14, while I was at the same house, the Spirit informed us that she could not speak freely in the night of August 9 because the behavior of the people had been so rude, but expressed her joy in discoursing with Christians. "You know," said I, "a thousand times more than any of us." "Yes, I do," said she. Abner Blaisdell said to me, "You stand too near her." Then I asked, "Do I stand too near you?" "No," said she, "stand as near as you please." I felt surprised and said it was a wonderful event. "Yes," the Spirit replied, "it is a wonderful event indeed—do you not remember what you told me just after I was married, that if I was married to Christ, how happy I should live?" "Yes," I answered, "I remember it very well." She exhorted the young people and told them that, without a change, they would be miserable. After this, the Spirit expressed her resolution to convince us that Abner Blaisdell and his family were clear of the evils alleged against them.

"They say I am a witch and a devil," said she, "and they said that Christ was a devil." The Spirit said other things, which I remember not.

At last she told them she was about to appear in order to convince them. Then by her direction we went up, and having prayed together, and heard the token, we walked on to James Miller's, singing the 84th Psalm. I was one of the foremost of the company and did not see it then, but the greatest number of those who were behind me said they saw it plainly.

When we were at James Miller's house, we stood in the field, while Lydia Blaisdell, in great fear, walked with the Spirit before us,[34] a few rods toward Samuel Simpson's, and then returned and told us that we must walk back, two and two, to her father's house singing, and the Spirit would follow us back. We did so. Richard Downing and I walked behind all, except Lydia Blaisdell, in order if possible to see the apparition. When we had walked about fifteen rods, I saw a white appearance forward of us to the left hand. As we passed by it, it fell in after us and walked with Lydia Blaisdell.

Richard Downing and I turned and looked upon them and heard them talk. We walked a little way further, stopped and looked upon them, and heard them talk again, but they spoke with so low a voice we could not understand them. The Spirit appeared in a personal form, white as snow, about as tall as Lydia Blaisdell.

It was now daybreak. I turned my eyes from the object, and in half a minute looked toward it again, but it was gone. Richard Downing then told me he saw it disappear.
–Paul Simpson

### TESTIMONY OF MR. SAMUEL INGALLS

August 13—14, 1800. I was at the house of Abner Blaisdell in the evening, with about forty people, went into the cellar with a candle, which discovered to us the whole cellar, so that no person here could be concealed from us. The light being put out, we heard a knocking. It was spoken to, and a voice shrill and pleasant, like what I never heard before, answered (and talked with us). Richard Downing asked her if she knew him. She said, "Yes," and called him by name three times. She often uttered her sentences three times. He asked the Spirit if she had never been at his house. The answer was that she had been there once.

Captain Paul Simpson said, "You know as much as a thousand of us." "Yes, yes," she answered, "but it will not be long before some here will know as much."

Abner Blaisdell asked the Spirit when she experienced her change. She answered that it was on her deathbed and then uttered the words, "Glory, glory, glory. Alleluia."

After some silence, some person asked the Spirit, "Are you about to leave us?" She answered, "I must go when Jesus calls. I must appear and walk with you this night, but you must walk in order. I will walk behind with Lydia," and told us that she had walked with her before.

"If you do," said Lydia Blaisdell, "I shall faint away."

"No," said the Specter, "you shall not faint again," and then said to the people, "If she faints again, don't you believe me.[35]

Lydia Blaisdell never fainted after this. We went to James Miller's and stood there. Lydia Blaisdell walked, as I was told she was before ordered, several rods from us, and I saw something appear white by her side, but no personal form. I heard Lydia Blaisdell say that, when the Spirit was with her and talked with her, she was not so much afraid as when she expected her coming.  –Samuel Ingalls

### TESTIMONY OF MR. JAMES SPRINGER

August 13, 1800. After much conversation with the Specter, she told us that she must talk and appear at the house of James Miller because he had reported that she could not be anywhere but at Abner Blaisdell's house. "And Lydia must walk with me," said she, "that you may all see that she is one person and I another."

We walked in order to that house, and I saw the Spirit as plainly as ever I saw any person. I saw the Spirit appear and disappear several times that night.[36]  –James Springer.

### TESTIMONY OF MR. JOHN SIMPSON

August 8, 1800. I heard the discourse of the Specter· in company with about thirty other persons. The sound of her voice was sometimes hoarse and faint, but for the most part it was clear and free from any impediment, and then it was inimitable, and the most delightful that ever I heard in my life. In discoursing with her parents, she said, "My dear parents, if the Lord should call you to go away with me this night, are you willing?"

"I fear I am not," said her father, "but the Lord can make me willing."

"Yes," she answered, "and none but he."

While Thomas Urann was talking with her, he observed that there were among us various distinctions of Christians, as Baptists, Presbyterians and Methodists, and asked which of these are right. "There are good and bad of all of these sorts," said she, "for the elect's sake." Mr. N. H. expressed his desire to handle her. "Handle me and see," said she, "for Christ tells you that a Spirit hath not flesh and bones." Accordingly, after it was broad daylight, and we could all plainly see each other, the outer cellar door being open, he extended his arms around the space in which the voice was then speaking, and exclaimed, "Oh, there is nothing here." The voice and this experiment were about four feet from me, so that I am sure that no living person could be concealed from me.[37] –John Simpson

### TESTIMONY OF MR. RICHARD DOWNING

August 9, 1800. I went to the house of Abner Blaisdell with a number more. After sometime we heard a knocking. Then four persons with me went into the cellar. A light was called for and brought. We searched the cellar to see if no person or thing might be found there whence that knocking might proceed. Then the light was carried up, and immediately there was the sound of knocking. Abner Blaisdell and Benjamin Downs several times asked what was wanted. At length a voice answered, that, if we would all go into the cellar, we should be satisfied; we then all went down.[38] There was then, in my hearing, much disorder and much profanity among the people. Nothing remarkable being heard, all but three or four of us left the cellar. Then again there was a knocking several times. We spoke, but obtaining no answer, I also went up.

Soon after I was informed that the voice had spoken to those who remained there, declaring that we must all return, and we went again. Immediately, there was a knocking all round the cellar by several persons there, as they afterwards owned to me. Abner Blaisdell desired them to be peaceable and give room. After a few minutes, Benjamin Downs expressed his sorrow that so many should be deceived and advised us to pray and return home. We therefore returned as unsatisfied as we went.

On the 13th, while I was very much engaged in business, I felt very much concerned for Abner Blaisdell, on account of his troubles, and thought I would go and see him, and advise him to a settlement, to prevent the expense of the law. I went, and he asked me the cause of my coming. I answered, to visit him as a friend. "I am glad to see you," said he. "You went away the other night very unsatisfied. You did not then appear to be afraid. Would you not be daunted now?" I told him I did not think I should. "Providence," said he, "has sent to here, I believe, and you must tarry all night." I told him I would. Then he informed me that he had talked with the Spirit in the forenoon, which directed him to persuade certain people to come to his house. About an hour after sunset, the Specter knocked, and being addressed, answered, "I have come to satisfy you all. Who is now speaking to me?" It was answered, Abner Blaisdell. "Let him and everyone of this family," said the Specter, "go out from here."

They went out. The voice then said that Abner Blaisdell's family was all clear of what was alleged against them.

After this, the voice talked with me. To know what answer would be made, I asked, "To whom are you speaking?" It answered, "Richard Downing." I asked again, "Were you ever at my house?" It answered, "Yes, I was there once with my mother, Mrs. M. and others, when your wife was sick." I had not then told any person what the Specter now told me, and which I and my family know to be true. Her mother asked[39] how long before her decease, she experienced her change. She answered, "When I was on my deathbed."

Soon after the Spirit said to the whole company, "I will walk with you to the next house, if you will walk in order, two and two, singing a psalm as you go, for God is a God of order." I asked her what psalm we should sing?

"Any," said she, "which may suit best."

We then left the cellar, sang and prayed, and immediately the token was given by knocking. We then placed ourselves in order and walked on toward James Miller's house.

Anxious to unveil the deception, if there was any, I walked near those who were foremost and was first at the door and knocked. James Miller came to the door and asked what all this meant. I answered, they are come to visit you. Immediately, I went and stood on the trapdoor—the only door of the cellar—that no person might go into it without my knowledge. Some of the company told James Miller our design, and he made us welcome. Then hearing the miraculous sound under the floor, James Miller with others went down and talked with a voice, which I heard and understood not, but was informed by them that she told them she had come there to give evidence that she could be and talk at other houses, as well as that of Abner Blaisdell, and that if the company would properly stand in the open field, she would pass before them, so that they might see her. The company did so. The Spirit then appeared and walked back and forth, two or three times, in view of the company and by the side of Lydia Blaisdell. This my eyes saw. The apparition, with Lydia Blaisdell, having advanced a few rods, disappeared. Lydia Blaisdell then came and told us that, if we would return to Abner Blaisdell's house, she would walk behind us. The company complied. Having a desire so be as near the apparition as possible, I walked with Paul Simpson behind the whole company. Lydia Blaisdell walked behind Paul Simpson as she had been ordered by the apparition. When we had walked about twenty rods, Lydia Blaisdell said, "There it is now." "Where?" said I. "There," said she, pointing to the left side of the company forward. I looked there and saw the dark appearance of a person, and kept my eye upon it till we passed by it, and till I saw it come in next after me, and by the side of Lydia Blaisdell. Thus it followed us. But now this object was become as white as the light. As we walked, I kept my eye upon this object almost without intermission, that I might see it disappear. It followed us by one direct motion, like a cloud. The motion was not ambulatory in the least degree. In this manner the apparition followed us about twenty rods, and then disappeared in my view. It opened into two parts and vanished.

–Richard Downing


### TESTIMONY OF CAPTAIN SAMUEL SIMPSON

August 5, 1800. In the evening after I had prayed, I looked toward the opposite side of the room and saw a white personal form having on a woman's cap, and the same countenance and features which Nelly Butler had when she was alive and in health, so that I knew her immediately. "In the name of the Lord," said I, "for what purpose are you here?" But there was no answer. I spoke again—"In the name of the Lord Jesus Christ, who are you, and what do you want here?" My wife greatly surprised, and seeing nothing, asked what was the matter. I told her I saw an apparition. "No," she replied, "you are deranged. It is the moon you see."[40] At that moment the apparition disappeared. When we were composed, we agreed to mention the matter to no person, and we conducted accordingly.

Two nights after, Abner Blaisdell called us up about two o'clock and informed us that the Spirit had been at his house and sent him to call for more evidence. He desired that we would go with him to his house. "Well," said my wife, "she

appeared here the night before last." "Then perhaps she has performed the message before me," said Abner Blaisdell. We went to his house. Hearing nothing for some time, by the desire of Abner Blaisdell I prayed with the company who had collected there. Immediately after, we heard the usual sound on the side of the house. We all went into the cellar and heard an articulate voice unlike any sound which I ever heard before.
–Samuel Simpson


### TESTIMONY OF MRS. SARAH SIMPSON[41]

I can attest to the truth of what my husband has now related, and further, that when we were in the cellar, the spirit told us that she was once Nelly Hooper, Nelly Butler, repeating the words three times, "You have done right," said she. "You have united in prayer, and it is true what that man said, who made the prayer, he did see me with a cap on." I am sure Abner Blaisdell could have told no one of it, for we had not told him, nor had anyone else that the apparition had appeared with that article of dress. I asked the Spirit, "Are you from happiness or misery?" She replied, "I am from above. I am not from beneath. I have come on God's errand." Then she sung alleluias and mentioned the cherubim and seraphim. She told me that my child, whom I had lost, was in heaven, praising God with the angels. "I should have spoken to that man," said she, "the other night, if some person had not been frightened." I asked, "Who was it?" She answered, "It was his wife." Abner Blaisdell and James Miller asked several questions, and the answers were wonderful.

August 9–10. I tarried after the people in general went off with the opinion that the words of the Spirit were in reality the words of Lydia Blaisdell. I was much surprised with the sound of knocking, which made the house tremble. I then heard Lydia Blaisdell say, "If I am guilty, let her stay away. If I am clear, let her come and clear me." In a few minutes after, she arose from a bed on which she had sat, and stood wringing her hands in distress. "What have I done," said she, "that I must be accused of all this?"

"Nothing, dear, you have done nothing, but you must go into the cellar," answered a voice in a vacant space where no person was—a voice the most delightful that ever I heard.

Some of the people then told her that she must do as the Spirit had said. "So I must," said she. "If I don't, she will come into the room, and if she does, I shall die." She then went down with a number of others, and immediately came up, and told me that she was released. I was soon after informed that the Spirit was about to appear and that we must all be present. I went with the rest but prayed that I might not see her. She had promised that none should see her but those who desired it. Accordingly, I did not see her though I looked directly before me where they said that she was.

August 13. I was again at the same house, and while I was sitting in the room, near a candle, two persons came and looked upon a watch, and found it twelve, and said it was exactly what the Specter had just told. At one o'clock they came again and found the same agreement. –Sarah Simpson


### TESTIMONY OF MRS. ABIGAIL ABBOTT

August 9, 1800. I was at Abner Blaisdell's house, with many more. In the first part of the night there was much indecent conduct and some profanity. The Spirit knocked sometimes but uttered only a few words. The company in general, having in vain waited to see or hear something extraordinary, withdrew, but I tarried with several other persons. Soon after they were gone, the Specter knocked several times very loud, and we went into the cellar. After saying many things to us, she appeared in the shape of a person and moved before us, without stepping, passing and re-passing several times. She gave so much light that we could see other persons and other things in the cellar which we could not see before her appearance, nor afterwards. I saw her appear and disappear several times. At last the apparition came to Captain George Butler, and then he appeared to be immersed in her radiance so that he appeared white and shining like the apparition. And I did particularly see his hand in the midst of the apparent body of the apparition. He cried in surprise, "Lord Jesus Christ."

August 13–14, I was there again and heard much conversation of the ghost, with several other persons in the cellar, concerning several events known only to her and them in her lifetime. To all their questions she gave satisfactory answers.

Once while she was speaking, I saw a bright shining appearance in that part of the space from whence the voice proceeded.

Her conversation and exhortation continued four hours. One of the company observed to her that we were a hardened people. "Yes," she answered, "but the Lord will call in his elect in his own time." I went to James Miller's with the company but did not then see her at all.  –Abigail Abbot


### TESTIMONY OF MRS. DORCAS ABBOT

I can attest, as an eye and ear witness, to all that is declared under August 9th, in the last testimony. I plainly saw George Butler's hand go through the apparition. –Dorcas Abbot


### TESTIMONY OF MR. FREDERIC HOUSOFF

I was an eye and ear witness of all the facts declared in the last testimony, and can attest particularly that I plainly saw George Butler put his hand on the apparition and saw his hand pass through it, glowing with the light of. –Frederic Housoff

### TESTIMONY OF MR. JOSEPH BLAISDELL

I was present when the important transaction took place on the night of August 9, 1800, and saw George Butler's hand pass through the body of the apparition, while he uttered the words, "Lord Jesus." He afterwards informed me and others that, while his hand passed through the breast of the Specter, he felt nothing. –Joseph Blaisdell


### *Testimony of Captain Paul Blaisdell*

I have seen and discoursed with the apparition several times. In the latter part of January 1800, I saw her in the field, first at a considerable distance from me. Then she came to me, and I particularly observed that she never touched the ground. Her raiment appeared as white as possible. The next evening she reproved me in the hearing of several persons because I had not spoken to her, and because I had spoken against her. She told me she had come on God's errand and that, if I opposed her, I opposed him who sent her.

The Spirit asked me if I lived in such a manner as I would wish to die.[42]

I have from time to time heard the voice speak in open space, where I am sure no living person existed, as others can testify who were with me.[43]

August 3, I saw her again and heard her pious discourse with nearly twenty other persons.[44] To those who were present, I said, "She has her child now in her arms."

"Yes, I have," she answered. "Yes I have." She came so near to me and others that either of us could have handled her without changing our places.

And upon August 9–10, I was present and saw the Specter when she appeared, and I plainly saw George Butler's hand pass through the apparition.

August 13. Being informed that the ghost had promised to come this night, I left my father's house and went to James Miller's that I might not see nor hear her. Just before daylight, she came to this house with more than forty people and reproved me again for speaking against her in the presence of six or seven persons. "This is the second time," said the voice, "that you have been warned. Beware of the third time." She asked me several times to handle her, to see whether she had material substance or not. I confessed to her that I believed her to be the spirit of Nelly Hooper. Then I went back with the company to my father's house. Before she vanished, she came and stood within three feet from me.[45] The personal shape was all light, the particles of which had constant motion. But I was afraid to put my hand upon her.   –Paul Blaisdell

### TESTIMONY OF MR. DAVID HOOPER

January 2, 1800. By the request of the Specter, sent by two messengers, I went to Abner Blaisdell's house, and by conversing with her, obtained such clear and irresistible tokens of her being the Spirit of my own daughter, as gave me no less satisfaction than admiration and delight.[46]

She gave a reason satisfactory to me why she put me to the trouble of coming there instead of her coming to my house. By her request I went in a few days after to George Butler's family and expressed my conviction to them.

August 8, I was there again with my wife and many others. I again asked the ghost who she was. The voice answered, "I was once Nelly Butler, your dear child. If the Lord should call you this night, are you willing to go with me?" I said the Lord can make me willing. "Yes," she replied, "and none but he." Then she mentioned certain articles of property which she had left, as belonging to us. "I hope," said I, "these matters do not disturb you." "No, no," she answered, "No, no. Peace. There must be peace."   –David Hooper

Her next words were spoken to me in particular. "Do you not remember what I said on my deathbed?"

I answered, "Yes, I do remember that you then said you desired peace while you lived."

"Yes, I did," said she, "yes I did." Sometime before this the Specter had sent this token to me, which, though not certain, had yet been attained with such circumstances as rendered the use of it for deception utterly improbable.

August 13, we went again. The Spirit then asked if we wanted to see her, and we both said no. "Did I ask you in your last sickness," said I, "whether you was willing your child should live?" The voice answered, "Yes, yes, and I told you I should be a vile creature to desire the life of the child." (For that was the time in which it was God's will it should die.[47]) I asked this question for further satisfaction, knowing that this very question and answer had passed between us.

The Spirit then told us that she had not freedom to converse on the night of August 9 by reason of disorder and profanity, and expressed her liberty and joy in discoursing with Christians. In the midst of her discourse with others, I silently indulged my painful reflections on the distress of her last sickness. Suddenly, I was surprised with these words of the voice to me: "Mourn not for me, for I am a happy soul."

Paul Simpson observed that her free conversation with us was a great wonder. "Yes, a miracle," said she, "such as never was since Christ was upon earth."[48] When she had told us that, without a change of heart, mankind would be miserable, I desired Abner Blaisdell to ask her when she experienced her own change. He asked, and she answered, "When I was on my deathbed." Richard Downing proposed this question: "Do I believe that you are such as you profess to be?" Her reply was, "You have believed, and you have not believed, and Satan will tempt you again."[49] Then he asked, "Were you

100

ever at my house in your lifetime?" "Yes, once, yes, once," said she. I knew the time of this visit, for Mrs. M. and I were there with her. By my desire, therefore, Richard Downing asked, "Who was there with you?" "My mother and Mrs. M.," said she, "when your wife was sick." Then Richard Downing told the people that he remembered she had been there at that time. "Have you been anywhere but here?" said he, "since your death?" "Yes," she answered, "to five places."

Abner Blaisdell's family being now excluded from that apartment where the Spirit was, she told us that Abner Blaisdell's family were innocent. "They say I am a witch and a devil," said she, "and they said that Christ was a devil. It is reported that some of this family have raised me, but it is not in the power of man or devil to fetch a soul from heaven."

After much more conversation the Spirit told us that she would walk with us to James Miller's, and to another house beyond it, but she only walked with us to James Miller's, and there talked with him and Paul Blaisdell to convince them who she was.

When we had come within twenty rods of the house, the company stopped. Then we two looked round and saw a white shining appearance by the side of Lydia Blaisdell, and about as tall as she.[50] After this, we observed nothing worthy of particular notice. –Joanna Hooper


### TESTIMONY OF EUNICE SCAMMONS

August 3, 1800. I was at the house which the ghost had so often visited, and was one of seventeen people or more who were present when she appeared and conversed with us.[51] After she had discoursed particularly with several persons, she said, "I am the voice of one crying in the wilderness, prepare ye the way of the Lord and make his paths strait. But you, who are sinners, do not make them strait. Some of you say that I am not a spirit, others, that I am an evil spirit. The words which I have spoken unto you have been mis-improved, perverted, and turned to ridicule. But I shall see you all when you will not laugh."

In the intervals of conversation, she sang praises.

Being asked who she was, she said, "I was once Nelly Hooper, and when I died, I was Nelly Butler," and mentioned several circumstances which attended her death to confirm her declaration.

After much other conversation, she appeared in the midst of us and talked while she appeared. She came so near me that I could have laid my hand upon her. She had before solemnly entreated us to stand round separate and in such order that all might see her while she moved in the midst of us.[52] Within our two ranks she slowly passed and re-passed from end to end three times, and passed by me six times. There were several persons in the company dressed in white, but I could not see them at all, while the Specter was as white as anything could possibly be. She moved in such nearness to every one of us, that everyone might have handled her. I saw her vanish instantly in the midst of us. After this, she spoke to us again by exhortation. "I am sent," said she, "to warn you against sin. I was myself a great sinner when I lived in this world. In my last hours, I received mercy. But if you go on in a course of sin and waste your time as I did, it may not be so with you. One half hour now gives me more happiness than this whole world can give you through your whole lives."

It was now daylight, and she observed to us that it was the Lord's Day, that we must retire to our homes and keep it holy. She desired Abner Blaisdell to pray with us before we parted.

After many other words, she left us singing alleluias to God and the Lamb. I heard the voice of her praises sounding further and further from us for a considerable time before it entirely ceased uttering the words, "Alleluia, alleluia. Glory, glory to God and the Lamb." Her notes were solemn and exceedingly delightful. Then we all went up, and Abner Blaisdell's prayer was our dismission. –Eunice Scammons

### TESTIMONY OF MRS. MARY BRAGDON

Sometime in January, 1800, I was at the house of Abner Blaisdell, and heard such a voice as I never heard before among the living, and they told me it was that of the Spirit, talking with George Butler and Lydia Blaisdell.

August 7. At the same house we heard a knocking on the partition next to the chimney, where no person could be. Then several persons with me went into the cellar, and the Spirit told us she was once Nelly Butler. She told me that I must not be scared.

August 13. I was again at the house with forty-eight others, besides children. The Spirit, after her conversation with several persons, exhorted the youth. "I was once young and vain as you," said the voice, "and, if the Lord had taken me away in that condition, how miserable I should have been! Now is the time, while you are young, to seek the Lord. Delay not till it is too late." Then it was that I saw a white personal form shining in the space from whence the voice proceeded, and I afterwards saw the same appearance in the field.
–Mary Bragdon

### TESTIMONY OF MRS. DORCAS JOHNSON

I was present at the house, and at the time it dated, August 13, by other testimonies. There I heard and saw the Specter. Her voice was distinct from any other, and her music the most delightful that I ever heard. When she walked with us, she moved without stepping. And when we arrived at the house, by direction of the Specter given to my brother, James Springer, and by him to the company in our hearing, we opened to the right and left, so that the Specter and Lydia Butler passed together between our two ranks. Then she vanished from my view, and I saw her no more. –Dorcas Johnson

***

# Two 19ᵀᴴ Century Retellings

***

FROM THOMAS FOSS, *A BRIEF ACCOUNT OF THE EARLY SETTLERS ALONG THE SHORES OF THE SKILLING'S RIVER, INCLUDING WEST SULLIVAN, WEST GOULDSBOROUGH, TRENTON POINT, AND NORTH HANCOCK.* ELLSWORTH, ME: N.K. SAWYER, 1870. 14-17.

Since the "Salem Witchcraft" nothing of a local nature has created such a furor of excitement, in this vicinity, as the, so called, 'Blaisdell Spirit' affair, which occurred in Sullivan, A.D. 1800. The limits of my book forbid anything more than a cursory mention; but the curious are referred to a book containing the full account, published about that time, by the Rev. Mr. Cummings, a learned minister of the gospel. [14]

Dr. Cotton Mather believed that the Evil One was at work in Salem, and vindicated the burning of the witches; so Mr. Cummings, with all his great learning, was a firm believer in the 'spirit,' and wrote his book to convince unbelievers. A reprint of this book has recently been made by the spiritualists of Portland Me.

The whole thing 'in a nutshell,' was something like this:--A young man loses his wife by death; being rather good looking, a certain spinster resolves to 'catch him alive' for a husband.[1] Her love not being reciprocated, she visits the celebrated Moll Pitcher, in Boston, returns, and, with the aid of some confederates, commences operations. And now comes the wonderful part. The affair assumed a phase which astonished and terrified even the original projectors of the scheme.

Making due allowance for the ignorance, superstition, and easy credulity of a large class of the population in those days, many things, it must be admitted, then transpired, which cannot be explained, if they are independent of demoniac agency. With one anecdote, of the hundreds which might be told, we will drop the subject.

Mr. John Urann was a man always ready for a joke. One day, while at work getting hay on the west side of Sullivan Falls, he was told that the 'spirit' was to appear that night at Mr. Blaisdell's, on the opposite side. Hurrying through his work he recrossed before night, went home, told his wife, (an unbeliever) where he was going and requested an early supper. But, 'no' said she, 'not a mouthful of supper shall you have if you are going up there!" So off John went, tired and hungry as he was.

Arrived at Mr. B's he found a crowded house; for the excitement through the community was then at a fever pitch. Elbowing his way through the crowd, he got near as he could to Mr. B. and heard him say 'she knocks; speak to her.' This was addressed to his daughter, the spinster, to whom we have before alluded. [15]

John listened and thought he could imitate the raps, so slipping out unobserved, he fixed a shingle into his bosom, and by rapping upon this with his knuckles, he found to his delight, that he could produce a good imitation of the hollow knocking sound, which proceeded from the cellar.

Creeping through an outside window, he curled himself down in the darkness, and rapped upon his shingle.

"She knocks," said Mr. B. "speak to her." But the medium was not deceived. "Father," said she, "that is not the spirit, someone must be in the cellar."

So, lights were procured, the cellar searched, the "unbelieving infidel" fished out, and all went "merry as a marriage bell;" but John soon found means to return to his former position, and again attempted to deceive them, when the medium declared that the spirit had left, and would not return until the intruder should be expelled. A Mrs. Gordon begged John to go up to her house, where he would find a plenty of good things to eat, and a nice bed.[2] This was too good an offer to be declined, so he left; the spirit of the departed lady did not appear again that night.

I spoke of the superstition and ignorance of a portion of the community in those olden times.

Many families believed in witches and fairies; and several old women were said to be witches. [16]

FROM AMBROSE SIMPSON, *SOME INCIDENTS OF A REMARKABLE REFERENCE CASE, CONNECTED WITH SOME OF THE INCIDENTS OF THE BLAISDELL SPIRIT THAT CREATED A GREAT SENSATION ABOUT THE TOWN OF SULLIVAN, COUNTY OF HANCOCK, ABOUT THE YEAR 1800.* BAR HARBOR: JOB PRINT, 1891. 16-19

About the year 1800 the inhabitants of this and surrounding towns were very much startled by a *spook* or what was called the *Blaisdell Spirit* which appeared for quite a long time at the house and farm of Abner Blaisdell, the farm on which so many stone wharves and roads are, and is now occupied by John D., a grandson of Abner Blaisdell, who at that time had a family of five sons and two marriageable daughters. The Spirit first made its appearances round about a chamber in the house, where in those primitive times the females of the family were engaged in sorting and picking fleeces of wool, by rapping three times, just as was done by the Rochester knockings forty years later; Sullivan is a fast town, it was about 40 years ahead of that spiritual manifestation and is as much more ahead in a reference award. The talk about the Blaisdell spirit became general in this and the surrounding towns and all over the county, and people came from long distances to witness its manifestations. Abner Blaisdell was a religious man and his house became famous as a resort for meetings of prayer and singing and hearing the knockings. Two Orthodox ministers, one Abram Cummings, who was celebrated for his ability and learning at that time, and one Benjamin Downs bestowed [16] a considerable part of their time in meetings, and trying to draw out what the mission of the spirit from Heaven was, as in its manifestations it claimed to come from there, and had a mission that it would at a future time divulge; there was a division of sentiment among the people who went to those meetings; a portion were tenacious in their belief that it was a spirit from heaven, while another portion of them thought it came from a lower region, but all acknowledged that it possessed a wonderful power, and did some unaccountable things. My father told in my hearing, when a young man, that at one of those meetings, at the Blaisdell house, his chair was against a clothes press door, that before the close of prayer, he heard three distinct raps on the inside of it, and at the close of the prayer, he opened it and removed all the articles there and could not find a hole or any way by which those raps could have been made by human agency; another incident of its manifestation was that of its rapping at Josiah Simpson's house on the Falls point, three miles away from the Blaisdell spirit house, the place of its principal operations; there was no turnpiked road here at that time, nor telegraph or telephone. It was soon after Simpson and his wife had retired to bed, that the raps were heard by both of them, his wife saying, "What is that noise?" when the sea captain replied, "It is Blaisdell's damned spirit down here." The remarkable part was that within fifteen minutes from the time of its being down there it was told so that several people who were assembled at the Blaisdell house heard it relate, that it had been to Josiah Simpson's and he swore that it was Blaisdell's damned spirit there and several person noted the time which proved to be just about the time that the rappings was heard by Capt. Simpson and wife, three miles away.

It was frequently announced by the spirit that at a future time it would make known its mission, and there was great anxiety to know; a night was set when it would appear and satisfy the inquiring mind, so a large congregation assembled at the house in hopes to learn more about it, my father one of them, so after prayer and singing they waited; sang more hymns and still waited and waited; the house and even the cellar was filled with people, but no rappings or other manifestations were obtained; at length those who had no faith in its being a good spirit began to [17] knock on his own account, and they caught one another by the arms while knocking, and they turned the affair into a *spree* and left, concluding the spirit had deceived them and *would lie*; after the exodus some believing persons remained there and said the spirit appeared and gave as a reason that it didn't appear before was there was so many wicked ones there that it would not appear.

At another meeting at headquarters, at the Blaisdell House, it was proposed that the congregation form and walk in twos to the next farm and neighbors house, Capt. Millers, for an evening meeting, as they proceeded there was a specter apparently, a woman dressed in white or with a white mantle over her, by the side of and not far from the congregation as they walked along; at that time it was said that Minister Downs and a resident by the name of Downing walked together, and seeing the apparition the following colloquy passed between them. Says Mr. Downs, "Do you see the spirit? Well take hold of it." "No," said the other, "you are a preacher of the gospel you take *right hold* of it." "No," said Downs, "you are an older man you take hold of it." So they let the opportunity slip, but it was said that during the services that evening at Capt. Miller's, that notwithstanding the cellar doors were closed and the apparition was not seen to enter the house, there was frequent rapping from the cellar and all over the house. Many more incidents took place but time and space will not admit them here. It stalked about quite a length of time and finally made known its mission, that George Butler marry the oldest daughter Lydia, which he did; and the younger daughter conceived, though she said it must have been by the Holy Ghost as there was no other cause; and as it passed away in infancy it will never be known whether it had power to work miracles.[3]

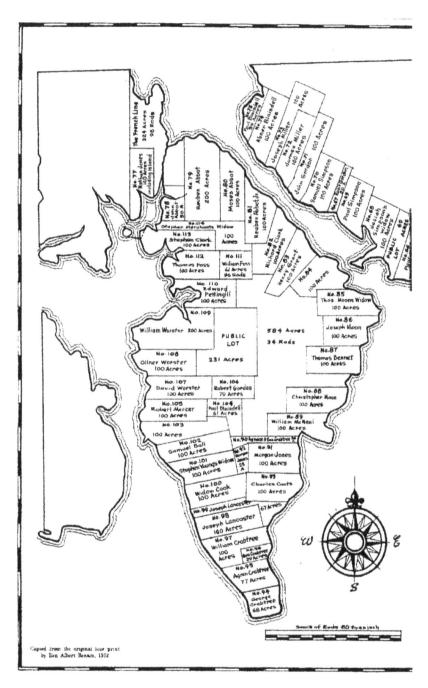

1803 Map of Sullivan, Maine
Reproduced with permission of the Maine State Museum.

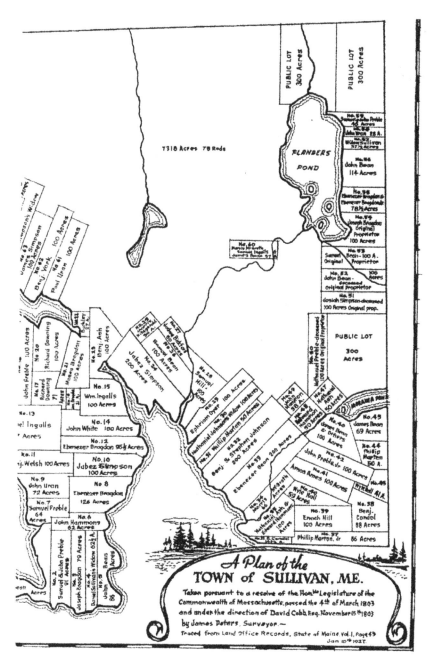

1803 Map of Sullivan, Maine
Reproduced with permission of the Maine State Museum.

113

# GENEALOGICAL MATERIALS

## BLAISDELL FAMILY

**The household of Abner and Mary Blaisdell, into which Lydia Blaisdell was born.** Adapted from the genealogy of the Blaisdell family assembled by Lois Crabtree Johnson, Hancock, Maine. [1]

**Abner Blaisdell**, yeoman, born circa 1752 York, Maine, deceased circa 1830-1840. He married **Mary Card**, daughter of Joseph Card; his second wife was **Hannah Simpson**, born 12 September 1748 or 14 November 1756, date of decease unknown. Abner served in the American Revolution.

**Children,** all born in Sullivan:
**i. Abner Blaisdell, Jr.**, yeoman, born 1774, deceased circa 1850-1860. He lived in Sullivan and never married.
**ii. Paul Blaisdell**, sea captain in 1800, farmer in 1850 census, born 1775, Sullivan, Maine, deceased circa 1850-1860. In June 1801 he married Margarett (Peggy) Miller, born 5 Sept. 1764, deceased 19 Sept. 1842. They lived in Sullivan and had four children.
**iii. Hannah Blaisdell**, born 1780, deceased 9 August 1840, Brewer, Maine. In May 1808 she married Atherton Oakes, born 20 May 1765. They lived in Hancock and moved to Brewer. She was his second wife. They had at least four children.
**iv. Joseph Blaisdell**, farmer in 1850 census, born 5 November 1784, deceased 31 December 1856, Sullivan, Maine. In December 1815 he married Elizabeth (Betsy) Donnell, born 1788, deceased 1867. They lived in Sullivan and had four children.
**v. Lydia Blaisdell**, born 1785, deceased in childbirth March 1801, Franklin. On 28 May 1800 she married George Goodwin Butler, born 6 June 1771, deceased 20 April 1826. They lived in Franklin, at Butler's Point, and had no surviving children.
**vi. Samuel Blaisdell**, born 1786, deceased circa 1860-1870. He married first wife Mary Elizabeth Mercer, born 1791, deceased 1829. They lived in East Franklin, and had eight children. He married second wife Mary Preble Donnell, born 1786, deceased 1858, sister to Betsy Donnell, wife of Joseph Blaisdell.
**vii. Ebenezer Blaisdell**, born 1786, deceased circa 1860-1870. Listed in census reports as "insane," he never married.

# HOOPER FAMILY

**The household of David and Joanna Hooper, into which Nelly Butler was born.** Adapted from the genealogy of the Hooper family assembled by Lois Crabtree Johnson, Hancock, Maine.

**David Hooper**, yeoman, born 26 February 1746, Saco, Maine, deceased circa 1814, Franklin, Maine. He married **Joanna Williams**, born circa 1755-1765, deceased 1824. David Hooper was a veteran of the American Revolution.

**Children,** all born in East Franklin:
**i. David Hooper Jr,** sea captain, born 1775, deceased 1836. In August 1804 he married first wife, Elizabeth Hardison. They lived in East Franklin and had six children. In August 1826 he married second wife, Rachel Jordan. They had four children.
**ii. Eleanor (Nelly) Hooper** born 25 April 1776, deceased 13 June 1797, on Butler's Point, Franklin, shortly after the birth and death of a child. Around 1795 she married George Goodwin Butler, born 6 June 1771, deceased 20 April 1826. They lived in Franklin, on Butler's Point, and had no surviving children.
**iii. Eliza Hooper** date of birth and decease unknown. She never married.
**iv. Sarah (Sally) Hooper** born 13 May 1778, deceased 3 May 1866. In December 1799 she married Moses Wentworth, yeoman, born 1777. They lived in East Franklin, on Egypt Stream, and had eight children.
**v. Abigail Hooper** date of birth and decease unknown. She never married.
**vi. Hart Hooper**, yeoman, born 9 August 1783, deceased circa 1850-1860. He married to Rebecca Maddocks, born circa 1784, Ellsworth, Maine, deceased circa 1850-1860. They had seven children.
**vii. John Hooper**, lumberman, born 9 July 1789, deceased 30 July 1854. In January 1821 he married Mary Harvey, born 21 September 1800, deceased 14 Oct. 1895. They had ten children.
**viii. Nathaniel Hooper**, yeoman, born 5 June 1795, deceased circa 1864. In June 1832 he married first wife, Avis Watts. In July 1849 he married his second wife, Eunice Buckley. They lived in Sullivan and had three children.
**ix. Joanna**, born 1784, deceased 20 November 1810. She married John Butler, born 25 June 1785, deceased 1845. They lived in Franklin and Hancock.

# BUTLER FAMILY

**The household of Moses and Sarah Butler, into which George Butler was born.** Adapted from the genealogy of the Butler family assembled by Lois Crabtree Johnson from Hancock, Maine.

**Moses Butler**, yeoman, born 22 February circa 1730, South Berwick, Maine, deceased 8 September 1817, Franklin, Maine, buried at Butler's Point, Franklin, Maine. He married **Sarah Goodwin**, born 1729, Kittery, Maine, deceased January 1806, Franklin, Maine. Moses Butler, regarded as the first settler of Franklin, served in the American Revolution and owned a saw mill.

**Children:**
**i. Mary Butler**, christened 24 February 1754, South Berwick, Maine, date of decease unknown.
**ii. Moses Butler, Jr.**, yeoman, born 17 February 1756, South Berwick, deceased 24 April 1839. In 1785 he married Mary (Polly) Moon, born 1760, deceased 1844. They lived in Hancock, or on Egypt Bay in Franklin, and had eleven children.
**iii. Sarah Butler**, christened 5 March 1758, South Berwick, Maine, date of decease unknown. In November 1778 she married Amaziah Goodwin. They never lived in Franklin, Maine.
**iv. Peter Butler**, yeoman, born 1761, South Berwick, deceased 17 March 1838. In 1787 he married Sarah Springer, born 1759, deceased 1848. They had six children.
**v. Nathaniel Butler**, yeoman, christened 25 Sept. 1764, South Berwick, Maine, deceased 18 April 1856. He married Hannah Springer (sister of Sarah Springer). They had eleven children.
**vi. Mercy Butler**, born 1767, Franklin, Maine, deceased August 1825. In December 1788 she married David Springer, born 22 January 1764, deceased 1847.
**vii. George Goodwin**, sea captain, born 6 June 1771, Franklin, deceased 20 April 1826, Franklin. Around 1795 he married first wife, Eleanor Hooper, born 24 April 1776, deceased 13 June 1797; they lived at Butler's Point and had no surviving children. In May 1800 he married second wife, Lydia Blaisdell, born 1785, deceased March 1801; they lived at Butler's Point and had no surviving children. In November 1805 he married third wife, Mary (Polly) Googins, born 11 March 1781, deceased 11 May 1862. They lived at Butler's Point and had eleven children. (Note: They named their first girl Eleanor.) George's Pond in Franklin, Maine, is named after George Goodwin Butler.

# CUMMINGS FAMILY

The household of Abraham Cummings, minister and writer who published the original account of the Nelly Butler hauntings. Except as otherwise noted, adapted from the genealogy of the Cummings family prepared by George Mooar, *The Cummings Memorial: A Genealogical History of the Descendents of Isaac Cummings, an Early Settler of Topsfield, Massachusetts.* New York: B.F. Cummings, 1903. 149-153.

**Abraham Cummings**, minister and writer, born 1754 (David Young and Robert Taylor, *Death Notices from Freewill Baptist Publications, 1811-1851*, 1985), deceased 31 August 1827 in Phippsburg, Maine, (death notice in Phippsburg newspaper on 13 September). In 1781 in Peterborough, New Hampshire, he married Phebe Thayer (lineal descendant of John Alden) born 11 February 1750, Braintree, Massachusetts, deceased 9 November 1795; married second wife, widow Hannah Leathe, from Watertown, Massachusetts, deceased March 1826. He received his AM degree from Rhode Island College (now Brown University) in 1776.

**Publications** include *Immortality Proved by the Testimony of Sense* (Bath, ME: Printed by J.G. Torrey, 1826) the original history of the Nelly Butler hauntings; *Spirits and Phantasms, The Two Witnesses* (Boston: Manning and Loring, 1797); *The Millennium* (Boston: Manning and Loring, 1797); *Contemplations on the Cherubim*, 1812; "The Present Times Perilous, A Sermon Preached at Sullivan on the National Fast, April 25, 1799" (Castine, ME: David J. Waters, 1799).

**Ministry** includes Bath in 1793 as supply pastor and in 1810 (US Census); Bucksport for six months in 1793 (*Bucksport Maine Churches*), 1794 ("Town Meeting Records" 1793, Vol. 1. 17; 1794, 25) and in 1800, when he organized a Baptist church (Millet, Joshua, *History of the Baptists in Maine*, 1845, 289); Freeport in 1790 (US Census) and in 1795 (Burrage, *History of the Baptists in Maine*, 103); North Yarmouth in 1796 as supply pastor and 1820 (US Census); Phippsburg in 1826; Sullivan in 1799, 1800, 1801, 1802, 1803, 1817 (*Book of Sullivan Town Records, 1789-1831*); Winthrop before 1800; Vinalhaven in 1805 where he organized first church (Millet 267; Burrage 146-47).

**Children:**
**i. Phebe Cummings**, born August 1783, deceased 23 March 1874. In December 1803 she married Isaac Bailey of North Yarmouth, Maine, deceased 21 September 1821. They had seven children.
**ii. Ebenezer**, sea captain, married but had no children.
**iii. Jabez**, deceased at approximately ten years of age.

❄❄❄

## GEORGE BUTLER'S LAST WORD

❄❄❄

In March 1801, soon after the funeral of his child bride Lydia Blaisdell, George Butler placed all of her possessions in a boat, set them on fire, and sent the burning boat out with the tide from Butler's Point.[1] In its journey to the sea, the burning boat directly passed the Blaisdell House, the principal setting of the Nelly Butler hauntings. George Butler's act would have far-reaching ramifications, even leading to the dissolution of the first church formed in the area.

Certainly, a distraught state of mind could have motivated the burning of Lydia's possessions. George Butler saw his second wife and child die in exactly the same manner as his first wife and child. This devastation was all the more horrifying since the Nelly Butler apparition had predicted Lydia's death ten months earlier. Yet the action of burning Lydia's possessions also suggests a certain abhorrence—a powerful statement on perceived fraud or witchcraft. Whatever the case, the act deeply offended the Blaisdell family. Thereafter, Lydia's father, Abner Blaisdell, harbored ill will for George Butler. When George later joined the first church formed in the area, he never disclosed this fact although Abner was already a member. Then the history surfaced, and the church conducted its own investigation, eventually excommunicating George Butler. Abraham Cummings took sides with George Butler, and the dispute deepened, dividing the church for the next seventeen years. In the last entry of its records, the church cited the disputes over the incident of the burning boat as "a principal cause of its dissolution."

## BUTLER FAMILY LEGENDS ON THE BURNING

"The story goes that George was teased into marrying a second wife when she pretended to be the ghost of the first wife. After her death George put all her clothes on a ship, set it afire and floated it off Butler's Point." From Ketchem, Joy. "Butler Genealogy" in the Butler Files at the Franklin Historical Society.


## CHURCH RECORDS IN RESPONSE TO THE BURNING

*Records of the First Baptist Church, Sullivan, Maine, 1810-1897.* Originals in Watson-Potter Archive, Sullivan-Sorrento Historical Society, Sullivan, Maine.


NOVEMBER 8, 1817
The church met in Conference at the House of Mr. Paul Urann's—after the exercise of their mind—[...] Voted to send to sister churches for assistance with regard to dividing the church into three—the churches sent to are Gouldsborough and Steuben—Wishing them to attend on the six day of January next at nine o'clock at the House of Mr. Samuel Ingalls—after this council was sent to the church [which] thought advisable to lay before them the circumstance of Mr. G. Butler which had caused some aversion in the church, which had taken place before he made a profession of religion. Some thought the thing had aught to be looked into while others thought the church had nothing to do with it. [17]


MARCH 2, 1818
The church met at Mr. Stephen Clark's according to appointment—Mr. Peter Butler gave the committee satisfaction and likewise Mr. Thomas Urann—after this the result of the committee—the church tried to resolve things that existed in

the church but they could do nothing so everyone went his own way—until September 5, 1818. They assembled at the meeting house—after prayer concluded to send on as usual to the Lincoln association. Danl. McMaster should prepare the letter on to the association, stating the situation of the church, with regard to their trials. [29]

JANUARY 3, 1818

The Council, according to the request of the church, met at the house of Mr. Ingalls of Sullivan. The Council being convened [...] attended to the complaint brought against Mr. G. Butler, which they found him guilty which he would not make any acknowledgement. Then the Council advised the church to cut him off which they did. What he was cut off for was that he denied that he avulsed[1] his wife's clothes after her death. Nathaniel Robinson, Job Chadwick Clark. [28]

SEPTEMBER 4, 1818

...We have had a painful trial with regard to Elder Abraham Cummings, the way and manner in which he came, it has been calculated to divide the church, and we may say subdivide; moreover E. Cummings has come again, by the means our trials are increasing. We will not say that E. C. has done anything intentionally with us, but it has been calculated to affect us very humbly. We have thought we would not trouble the Association with it, but our situation is such that if the Association should not instrumentally help us, we as a church must inevitably sink into oblivion. If the Association should want to know the particular, they will have the goodness to call on E. N. Robinson, who was one of the Council last winter. We, therefore, solicit prayerfully your attention to this subject in our opinion the more the bitter because E.C. is here and will go

---

[1] Avulsed (to separate oneself radically from another person or thing by cutting off or severing all ties).

away before long. If he has done right, the public had aught to know it, if not, they had. --If the association should think it a matter that will come under their interpretation, they will do as a committee in three or four week at the congregation. [30]

OCTOBER 14, 1818
Meet according to adjournment: Prayer by E. Robinson

The council presented to attend to an inquiry into the matter of difficulties in the church; finding that, by the advice of a former council, Mr. George G. Butler has been excluded from the church, and fearing that there was not a thorough investigation [31] of the subject at that time by that Council, that the church be advised to reconsider the vote which excluded Mr. Butler and place him back into the church for a fair and a thorough trial. The church by this committee accepted the advice as above—Adjourned to Mr. W. Martin to meet at candle light in connection with the church, comm. Elder A. Cummings, being present, prayed.

E. Cummings absolutely refused to tarry with us while we proceeded to business, which is a matter of deep regret to us— attended to inquire into the state of difficulties existing in the minds of brethren in consequence of the *manner* of past attention to existing trials, viewing that our connection with the committee be no longer expedient. [The] connection was disposed by the mutual consent of the parties, and the committee of elders by the consent of the church committee proceeded to examine the matters of trial in the capacity of an advisory council and, after gaining the best light we could obtain on the subject. Adjourned to 7 o'clock in the morning.

OCTOBER 15, 1818
Thursday morning meet according to adjournment prayer by the moderator. The committee of elders, after weighing was

accorded manner, the of this church, in their present difficulties feel satisfied that they have cost their visibility as a regular church, of Christ, in good and wholesome standing. [32] We therefore advise they consider that to be their present state and proceed to organize on the ground which the old church occupies a church, or church viewing the same articles of faith and covenant as were received by the old church, we moreover state, brethren, that in our opinion the proceedings of Elder Abraham Cummings relative to this church, have been a principal cause of its dissolution. We further state that, if this our result and advice should meet your apportion,[2] we feel willing to be at your service or to be disunified and that you call for another council to assist you as shall we trust your wishes. [signed] Phineas Pillsbury Moderator. Enoch Hunting Clarke [33]

OCTOBER 26, 1822

The church met in conference as usual Elder William Johnson being present presided and prayed with us, after the church had related their impressions of mind. 1$^{st}$ The church voted to accept the following letter. [...]

Rev. and Dear Sir,

Two letters we understand have been sent to you as president of the Massachusetts Missionary Society, against Elder Abraham Cummings, the first accused him of disturbing the peace of this church by advocating the cause of open communion, the second letter informed you that on the 4$^{th}$ of September A.D. 1818 this church presented a letter to our association stating their tried situation, and requesting their help, and also that Elder Cummings was the criminal cause of the pretending ruin of this church, we consider it our

---

[2] Approtion—an apparent mistake for *approbation*, given the context of the word.

indispensable duty to announce that each of these three assertions in these two letters is incorrect, that we may not seem to withhold any fact respecting this affair we submit the following. Elder Cummings preached a sermon to us in favor of open communion about a year after the above letters were written; but it never was a cause of difficulty in this place. The first cause of our difficulty was this: Elder Cummings brought a complaint against one of the members of this church, which complaint some of the leading members said was ill founded, unreasonable, and unjust; and accordingly we passed a vote to reject it. [43]   At this time, many of the members were disaffected by reason of this vote, for they conceived that complaint was well founded, reasonable, and just. There began our great difficulty at this time. Elder D. McMaster, without the consent of the church, addressed a letter to our association requesting their help; accordingly a council of seven elders was chosen and when met, we received them by vote, and this council after some deliberation and less examination advised us to dissolve the church by vote, which we through ignorance did.  But thanks be to God through our Lord Jesus Christ, that our eyes have been opened to see how the cause of God has been injured in this church.  We now feel to acknowledge that Elder Cummings' complaint was just, and also that we have done very wrong; and believing it to be our indispensable duty, we have renounced the advice of the council, and have resumed our former standing, that the day may soon arrive, when there shall be no more a prickling brier on a grieving thorn, is the prayer of your brethren in the fellowship of the gospel.

P.S. you will please to present this our letter to your missionary board,

Rev. Thomas Baldwin.  Signed in behalf of the church, James Foster, Clerk.

ACKNOWLEDGEMENTS

This history on the Nelly Butler hauntings could not have been written without the generous support from the Trustees of the University of Maine System and without the efforts and expertise from a number of local organizations and individuals such as Emery DeBeck, Karen Blaisdell, Gerard NeCastro, Bernie Vinzani, Loni Levesque, Dan Barr, the Sullivan-Sorrento Historical Society, the Maine State Library, and Jeanne Vose and Laura Bean of the Merrill Library. Special thanks go out to Lois Crabtree Johnson, genealogist and local historian.

## Notes to THE NELLY BUTLER HAUNTINGS: AN UNSOLVED MYSTERY

[1] Cummings, Abraham. Section I. In Cummings, Abraham. 1826. *Immortality Proved by the Testimony of Sense: In Which Is Considered the Doctrine of Spectres, and the Existence of a Particular Spectre.* Bath, Maine: J.G. Torrey. 14.

[2] Cahill, Robert Ellis. 1983. *New England Ghostly Haunts.* Peabody, MA: Chandler-Smith. 38.

[3] Cummings, Abraham. Section III. In Cummings, Abraham. 1826. 38.

[4] Pomode, Frank. 1902. *Modern Spiritualism: A History and Criticism.* Vol. 2. London: Methuen. 179-201.

[5] Citro, Joseph. 1996. "The Machiasport Madonna." In *Passing Strange: True Tales of New England Hauntings and Horrors.* Boston: Houghton. 33.

[6] Simpson, Ambrose. 1891. *Some Incidents of a Remarkable Reference Case Connected to Some of the Incidents of the Blaisdell Spirit That Created a Great Sensation about the Town of Sullivan, County of Hancock, about the Year 1800.* Bar Harbor: Record Job, 16.

[7] Roll, Muriel. 1969. "A Nineteenth-Century Matchmaking Apparition: Comments on Abraham Cummings' *Immortality Proved by the Testimony of Sense.*" *The Journal of the American Society for Psychical Research.* Vol. 63. 396.

[8] Roll, Muriel. 1969. 409.

[9] Foss, Thomas. 1870. *A Brief Account of the Early Settlers along the Shores of the Skillings River Including West Sullivan, West Gouldsborough, Trenton Point, and North Hancock, and Reminiscences and Anecdotes of Old Times and Folks.* Ellsworth, ME: N.K. Sawyer. 14.

[10] Stevens, William Oliver. 1949. *Unbidden Guests: A Book of Real Ghosts.* London: George Allen. 269.

[11] Cummings, Abraham. Letter II. In Cummings, Abraham. 1826. 23.

[12] Cummings, Abraham. Letter II. In Cummings, Abraham. 1826. 23.

[13] Genealogy of the Hooper Family. *See* "Genealogical Materials" in the present edition.

[14] "Death Notice for Nelly Butler." 1797. *Eastern Herald and Gazette*

*of Maine.* 15 July.   Reported by James Hansen, ed. "Probate and Miscellaneous Notices from the *Eastern Herald and Gazette of Maine* of Portland: Supplemental Notices for 1797 and Notices for 1798." 169.

[15] Carter, Bruce. 1996. *Oblivion and Dead Relatives Downeast.* Ellsworth, ME: Downeast Graphics. 63. Confirming the identity of the three unmarked graves on Butler's Point are accounts from local residents and the former caretaker of the property.  George Butler's name appears on the headstone for the family in the Franklin Cemetery, but he is probably not buried there since he died on April 20, 1826, and the headstone was erected in 1855.

[16] Genealogy of the Blaisdell Family; Genealogy of the Butler Family. See Genealogical Materials in the present edition.

[17] Johnson, Lois Crabtree, genealogist.   Interview by the author. 28 March 2008.  Sullivan, Maine.

[18] Cummings, Abraham. Letter II. In Cummings, Abraham. 1826. 27.

[19] Cummings, Abraham.  Letter II. In Cummings, Abraham. 1826. 25.

[20] Cummings, Abraham. Letter II. In Cummings, Abraham. 1826. 27.

[21] Cummings, Abraham. Letter II. In Cummings, Abraham. 1826. 28.

[22] Cummings, Abraham. Letter II. In Cummings, Abraham. 1826. 28.

[23] In Cummings, Abraham. Letter IV. In Cummings, Abraham. 1826. 35-36.

[24] Anderson, Rodger. 1983. The Cummings Apparition." *Journal of Religion and Psychical Research.* Vol. 6, No. 3. 213.

[25] Anderson, Rodger. 1983. 213.

[26] Anderson, Rodger. 1983. 207.

[27] Anderson, Rodger. 1983. 213.

[28] Cummings, Abraham. Letter II. In Cummings, Abraham. 1826. 22.

[29] Genealogy of the Blaisdell Family.

[30] Testimony of Paul Simpson, Jr. In Cummings, Abraham. 1826. 44.

[31] Cummings, Abraham. Letter I. In Cummings, Abraham. 1826. 17.

[32] Anderson, Roder. 1983.  214.

[33] Foss, Thomas. 1870. 15.

[34] Simpson, Ambrose. 1891.  18.

[35] Anderson, Rodger. 1983. 214.

[36] Note by Abraham Cummings to Testimony of Sally Martin. In Cummings, Abraham. 1826.  45.

[37] See Deposition of George Butler and Testimony of Samuel Simpson. In Cummings, Abraham. 1826. 41, 61-62.

[38] Cummings, Abraham. Letter I. In Cummings, Abraham. 1826. 20.

[39] Testimony of Jeremiah Bunker.  In Cummings, Abraham. 1826.. 51.

[40] Testimony of Mary Gordon. In Cummings, Abraham. 1826. 48

[41] Testimony of Paul Blaisdell. In Cummings, Abraham. 1826. 65.

[42] Cummings, Abraham. Letter I. In Cummings, Abraham. 1826. 20.

[43] Cummings, Abraham. Letter III. In Cummings, Abraham. 1826. 29.

[44] Testimony of Abner Blaisdell. In Cummings, Abraham. 1826. 52.

[45] Testimony of Sally Wentworth. In Cummings, Abraham. 1826. 49.

[46] Testimony of Eunice Scammons. In Cummings, Abraham. 1826. 68.

[47] Cummings, Abraham. Letter IV. In Cummings, Abraham. 1826. 32.

[48] Cummings, Abraham. Letter I. In Cummings, Abraham. 1826. 20.

[49] Testimony of Sarah Simpson. In Cummings, Abraham. 1826. 63,

[50] Cummings, Abraham. Letter I. In Cummings, Abraham. 1826. 19.

[51] Cummings, Abraham. Letter II. In Cummings, Abraham. 1826. 24.

[52] Cummings, Abraham. Letter II. In Cummings, Abraham. 1826. 24.

[53] Cummings, Abraham. Letter II. In Cummings, Abraham. 1826. 24.

[54] Anderson, Rodger I. 1983.

[55] Anderson, Rodger I. 1983.

[56] Testimony of Abigail Abbott. In Cummings, Abraham. 1826. 63.

[57] Testimony of Abigail Abbott. In Cummings, Abraham. 1826. 63.

[58] Foss, Thomas. 1870. 14.

[59] Stevens, William Oliver. 1949. 262.

[60] Reference made by Josiah Simpson. In Simpson, Ambrose. 1891. 17.

[61] Testimony of Sally Wentworth. In Cummings, Abraham. 1826. 49. The specter quoted John 1:23.

[62] Testimony of Sally Wentworth. In Cummings, Abraham. 1826. 49.

[63] Testimony of Sally Wentworth. In Cummings, Abraham. 1826. 50.

[64] Cummings, Abraham. Section IV. In Cummings, Abraham. 1826. 72.

[65] Note by Abraham Cummings to the Testimony of Paul Simpson. In Cummings, Abraham. 1826. 57.

[66] Roll, Muriel. 1969. 406.

[67] Roll, Muriel. 1969. 406-407.

[68] No accounts from the first week of August 1800 refer to Lydia Blaisdell and George Butler present at spiritualist gatherings. Perhaps the newlyweds were away, perhaps they sought to avoid the whole public spectacle, or perhaps they were present but not included in the extracts of the eye-witness testimonies. The last recorded sighting of the Nelly Butler apparition, five years after Lydia's death, appears in Letter VI by Abraham Cummings.

[69] Testimony of Paul Simpson. In Cummings, Abraham. 1826. 55.

[70] Note by Abraham Cummings to the Testimony of Paul Simpson. In Cummings, Abraham. 1826. 55.

[71] Note by Abraham Cummings to the Testimony of Paul Simpson. In Cummings, Abraham. 1826. 55.

[72] Cummings, Abraham. Letter VI. In Cummings, Abraham. 1826. 35.

[73] Cummings, Abraham. Letter VI. In Cummings, Abraham. 1826. 35.

[74] Cummings, Abraham. Letter VI. In Cummings, Abraham. 1826. 35.

[75] Cummings, Abraham. Letter VI. In Cummings, Abraham. 1826. 35.

[76] Cummings, Abraham. Letter VI. In Cummings, Abraham. 1826. 36.

[77] Cummings, Abraham. Letter VI. In Cummings, Abraham. 1826. 36.

[78] Cummings, Abraham. Section IV. In Cummings, Abraham. 1826. 75.

[79] Note by Abraham Cummings to the Testimony of Paul Simpson. In

Cummings, Abraham. 1826. 55.
[80] Stevens, William Oliver. 1949. 261.

## Notes for LETTERS BY ABRAHAM CUMMINGS

[1] Mooar, George. 1903. *The Cummings Memorial: A Genealogical History of the Descendents of Isaac Cummings, an Early Settler of Topsfield, Massachusetts.* New York: B.F. Cummings. 150.

[2] Mooar, George. 1903. 152.

[3] Stevens, William Oliver. 1949. *Unbidden Guests: A Book of Real Ghosts.* London: George Allen. 261.

[4] Cummings, Abraham. 1797. *Spirits and Phantasms.* Boston: Manning and Loring; Cummings, Abraham. 1797. *The Millennium.* Boston: Manning and Loring.

[5] Cummings, Abraham. 1812. *Contemplations on the Cherubim.* Boston: John Eliot.

[6] Cummings. 1826. Except for Letter VI, the various closing addresses (e.g. "With unvaried sentiments of esteem, I continue yours") have been omitted. The title of Letter I, missing in the original edition, has been provided by the editors.

[7] Hosea 4-14. By Deists, Cummings refers to skeptics from the Enlightenment.

[8] *Note from the original text.* The personal pronouns *she* and *her* are here used with reference to the sex to which the ghost belonged in this world.

[9] Sheridan and Longinus, an 18th century model of rhetoric and an ancient writer on the sublime.

[10] Acts 9: 3-7; 22: 6-9.

[11] Acts 12: 1-17.

[12] Luke 2: 9-10.

[13] "Spectre." 1823. *Encyclopedia Britannica.* 6th ed. Vol. 19. Edinburgh: Archibald and Constable. 577.

[14] Date unknown, probably early in the spirit's manifestations, December 1799.

[15] *Editor's Note:* Stewart, Dugald. 1792. *Elements of the Philosophy of the Human Mind. Note from the original text.* On the distinction between the original and required perceptions of sight.

[16] January 1, 1800; the two persons were Lydia Blaisdell and her father, Abner.

[17] Night of August 13-14, 1800.

[18] The specter instructed the spectators in orderly fashion to proceed to the house of vocal disbeliever, Captain James Miller, while she followed with Lydia Blaisdell; the specter also appeared in the field beside Miller's house and at the back of the procession returning to the Blaisdell residence.

[19] The passage links members of the Enlightenment (ye Paines) to the

infamous secret society known as the Bavarian Illuminati (ye Illuminees). References are to Thomas Paine. 1794-1807. *The Age of Reason: Being an Investigation of True and Fabulous Theology.* 3 Vol. and John Robinson. 1797. *Proofs of Conspiracy, against All the Religions and Governments of Europe.*

[20] The reference is to the specter of Nelly Butler orchestrating the marriage of George Butler and Lydia Blaisdell.

[21] Night of May 29, 1800.

[22] January 1, 1800.

[23] The reference is to the response of Moses Butler (George Butler's father) to Abner Blaisdell and his daughter Lydia, on January 1, 1800 and at an earlier meeting between Abner and the Butler patriarch.

[24] Mystery surrounds the re-interment of Nelly Butler's child at the request of Nelly Butler's ghost. The purpose of digging up the grave was to move its contents closer to the remains of Nelly Butler so that the child would rise at her right hand on Judgment Day. The dead infant even appeared with the specter in some of its manifestations. The re-interment took place at Butler's Point in Franklin, Maine. The event probably took place soon after the mass sightings ceased in August, when Abraham Cummings collected most of his testimonies. Thus the autumn of 1800 emerges as the most likely date for the re-interment.

[25] The specter spoke with Abner directly, then using him and Lydia Blaisdell as messengers, the specter summoned Moses Butler, the father of George Butler, on January 1, 1800, and David Hooper, the father of Nelly Butler, on January 2nd, 1800.

[26] *Note from the original text.* To him she had before sent several messages by several persons of different families.

[27] *Note from the original text.* I hear your objection. "There was a reason for her being consoled. Make me believe, if you can, that, if her professed ignorance of the affair was real, the appearance and discourse of a ghost by her side, would not augment her fears and distress." But remember, dear sir, that experience in this case is the best teacher. More than thirty witnesses of both sexes, are against you; all declaring that, though at first the ghost excited terror, yet, after a little discourse with her, their fears were entirely dissipated, and succeeded by particular pleasure: so familiar and delightful was the mode of her address and conversation. At this time Abner Blaisdell heard the conversation distinctly, but saw nothing. His daughter both saw and heard.

[28] *Note from the original text.* This was ordered by the ghost.

[29] Lydia Blaisdell and her father met with David Hooper on January 2, 1800, and he went to the Blaisdell residence that day and spoke with the apparition.

[30] Abner Blaisdell's opposition to the alliance was no doubt based on

Lydia's being only fifteen years old, unusually young for a woman to marry in Downeast Maine at this time. The fact that George Butler was nearly twice her age only exacerbated the issue. The river Abner and Lydia crossed was the Taunton River.

[31] January 2, 1800; the messengers were Lydia Blaisdell and her father, Abner.

[32] David Hooper's testimony indicates that this took place on January 5, 1800.

[33] *Editor's Note:* The reference is to the slander and accusations made against Lydia Blaisdell, that she was either the author of a delusion or a witch conjuring a demon in order to dupe George Butler into marriage. *Note from the original text.* That all these reasons were assigned at *that juncture*, I pretended not to say. Probably they were not, but certain it is, that she expressed them all to her friends at different times.

[34] This vessel, moored in either the Taunton River or the Skillings River, in Sullivan, was headed for York, Maine, where the Blaisdells had relatives.

[35] The specter of Nelly Butler appeared in the house of Samuel and Sarah Simpson, neighbors to the Blaisdells, as well as the homes of Josiah Simpson, James Miller, and Abraham Cummings.

[36] Nearly fifty people, not forty, participated in the encounter on the night of August 13-14, 1800. See Testimonies of Abner Blaisdell, Mary Gordon, and Hannah Gatcomb.

[37] See note 14 above.

[38] August 13, 1800. See Testimony of Mary Card.

[39] *Note from the original text.* Voltaire, in his philosophical dictionary, treating the Bible and ghosts with equal ridicule, says that the latter, "used to hide away at the crowing of the cock." The same was the idea of Shakespeare in his ghost of Hamlet, "Adieu, the glow worm shows the morning to be near." But this, we now see, is not always the case. *Editor's Note.* Voltaire. 1765. *Voltaire's Philosophical Dictionary, for the Pocket.*

[40] *Note from the original text.* These two, by their own desire, had obtained a promise that they should not see her. There were several such instances at different times.

[41] Luke 9: 28-36. The three eye-witnesses were Peter, John, and James.

[42] The six witnesses out of eleven on the night of August 9-10, 1800, who saw the specter pass between them and who saw George Butler put his hand through the specter.

[43] August 13, 1800. See Testimony of Mary Card.

[44] Night of August 13-14, 1800. The specter led a procession of villagers to the house of the vocal disbeliever, James Miller. She also announced the plan to visit another house of Samuel Simpson, but

never carried this out on the urging of Lydia Blaisdell, worn out from the series of encounters that night.

[45] Clearly a misprint, the sentence reads, in the original edition, "It is *early* enough to treat any affair with derision when we have fully discovered what it is."

[46] Proverbs 14.6.

[47] *Note from the original text.* A place in the house most distant from that of the Specter.

[48] Night of August 9-10, 1800.

[49] August 6, 1800.

[50] While the date and circumstances of this prediction cannot be pinpointed, it may have taken place on the night of August 8-9, 1800, when more than 30 people assembled at the Blaisdell residence.

[51] Night of August 13-14, 1800, shortly before the specter's famous procession through the village.

[52] Æsop's fable of "The Cock and the Jewel." This edition substitutes in this sentence the word "solution" for the obscure term "pasara," in the original edition, a Spanish verb meaning to hasten or to make happen.

[53] No details survive regarding this litigation in the Hancock County records from the Supreme Judicial Court and the Court of Common Appeals from 1800-1801. A Grand Jury determined whether a case had sufficient evidence to go to trial, and no records were kept for cases turned down by this judicial body.

[54] None of the letters, depositions, and testimonies give further clarification of this prediction.

[55] See Note 25 above on the re-interment of the child.

[56] This probably took place outside the house on Waukeag Neck where Abraham Cummings stayed with his family.

[57] *Note from the original text.* This meeting was the wedding. He who is able to receive it, let him receive it. One infinitely greater than this Specter attended the marriage at Cana in Gallilee.

[58] Night of August 13-14, 1800. *Note from the original text* In about an hour after she appeared to forty of this assembly. But I must here also insert a particular observation of Benjamin Rush in his chapter of illusions; "When a person fancies that he hears voices and sees objects, which do not exist, he has these sensations alone. The voice supposed to be heard, says he, and the objects supposed to be seen, are never heard nor seen by two persons, even when they are close to each other." The inference then is certain, with respect to those witnesses, that no mental disease could be the true origin of their hearing and vision. *Editor's Note*: Benjamin Rush. 1812. *Medical Inquiries and Observation upon the Diseases of the Mind.* Chapter 15.

[59] See Testimony of Mary Card. In Cummings, Abraham. 1826. 54-55.

## Notes for TESTIMONY BY EYE-WITNESSES

[1] Cummings, Abraham. *Immortality Proved by the Testimony of Sense: In Which Is Considered the Doctrine of Spectres, and the Existence of a Particular Spectre.* Bath, Maine: J.G. Torrey. 38.

[2] Cummings, Abraham. Section III. In Cummings, Abraham. 1826. 38.

[3] In addition to their depositions, Paul Simpson and Sarah Simpson also submitted testimonies that follow.

[4] *Note from original text:* The next deposition was given by one who looks upon the whole scene to be a great deception, somehow or other.

[5] The original account incorrectly listed this date as August 11· 1800. Most likely, the events took place on August 3, 1800, a Sunday when there was no preacher in the town. See Testimony of Mary Gordon. The only other possible date would be August 10, 1800, the last Sunday before the disappearance of the specter, but this day is improbable since there was a preacher in the town, Benjamin Downs, and the accounts stated that the evening before was uneventful, which surely did not describe the night of August 9, 1800.

[6] This appears to be the first time George Butler encountered the specter, which took place on January 2, 1800.

[7] Night of August 9-10, 1800. *Note from the original text:* This only means that they were together at a little distance from the rest of the company in the same apartment.

[8] Cummings separated depositions from testimonies, which is why he didn't fold the preceding oaths into his organization of the accounts that follow—opponents and adherents of the specter. In a typographical error, the original edition stated that Cummings collected these depositions on August 6, 1800, which is impossible since the accounts refer to events as late as the night of August 9-10, 1800.

[9] Cummings, Abraham. Section III. In Cummings, Abraham. 1826. 41.

[10] *Note from the original text:* She then expressed not only her own feelings but those of the family. The idea of a Specter coming into the room, where they commonly were, was distressing to them, as already observed.

[11] *Note from the original text:* I find no evidence that these two went without others.

[12] "New Jerusalem." 1795. Words by Isaac Watts, music by Jeremiah Ingalls.

[13] *Note from the original text:* This experience is testified by all who saw and heard.

[14] *Note from the original text:* This, however, he denies, but suppose it were true, why was it improper that in his own house he should choose the place where he would stand? If they knew where he was, that was sufficient. On this testimony a few observations must detain

the reader. We are liable to be deceived two ways: by the appearance of truth where it is not, and by the appearance of deception where it is not. Did not such an occasion as this require order? The Specter was about to communicate to the assembly an important message. Could they enjoy the best advantage to hear and attend to it, while they were changing places, — crowding and interrupting one another? Is not a voice better understood by any auditory if there be some intermediate space between the speaker and hearer? What did they want a candle for, unless they wanted to be deceived? The Specter was white; so is a deceiver by a candle. The Specter told them the exact time of night; so could a deceiver by a candle. Did they want a candle in order to see her? They had learned, or might have learned already, that she could make herself as visible without a candle, as any person living could with it. Four nights before this, she appeared to fourteen persons in this very place, and six persons saw the hand pass through the apparition. Two nights before this, she appeared to about twenty people, forming an ellipsis, within which she slowly passed round so near the circumference several times, that everyone of them might have handled her with deliberation, and she had also expressed her desire to give satisfaction by this experiment. Therefore, it was not because she was afraid to be seen or handled, that Abner Blaisdell made this arrangement; but for reasons possibly unknown to us. But *probably* one of them was this: On the night of this testimony, August 13, it was one design of the Specter to confirm what was past, by conducting as she had before, May 28. That is by appearing only to two or three persons, while to all others in the assembly, though conversing with her, she should remain invisible. This, we are assured by the testimonies of Abigail Abbott and Joseph Blaisdell, was now informed. On the above May 28, a third person thought he saw her, but was not sure; for he supposed he might be deceived by some change of the candlelight. Hence we easily see that those two persons who saw her on this night of August 13, while she invisibly discoursed with the assembly, obtained more satisfaction for others, if not for themselves, that what they saw was reality, than if there had been a candle; especially if we consider that several women of the assembly were dressed in white.

[15] Hooper was Nelly Butler's maiden name.

[16] *Note from the original text*: He had said that Abner Blaisdell's family could not raise the Spirit anywhere but in their own house, as several testified.

[17] The original edition lists the date as August 4, 1800, a typographical error since August 3rd fell on a Sunday, the day of the week identified by Mary Gordon and other witnesses.

[18] Watts, Isaac. "Song 27: For the Lord's Day Morning." In Watts, Isaac. 1715. *Divine Songs: Attempted in Easy Language for the Use of*

*Children with Some Additional Composures.*

[19] Isaiah 40:3. *Note from the original text*: That is, that they heard the same words.

[20] *Notes from the original text*: There was not only this similarity in voice, but the same phrases, which she was accustomed to use, and which were peculiar to her in her life time, she uttered now, as several of her intimate acquaintances have informed me. Sally Wentworth had now an opportunity to hear the voice of Lydia and the voice of the Specter in the same time and place that she might have the best advantage to judge whether or not there was the least agreement between them. And that Lydia had never learned to utter two voices in the same minute, the one her natural voice, the other the dying voice of this woman's sister, appears from the certainty that, through all the time of the Specter's last sickness and death, Lydia was two hundred miles distant from her. When Sally Wentworth heard in the East Room that sentence of the ghost, "I am the voice of one crying in the wilderness," this was the only time in which the ghost uttered these words for that day, as several witnesses declare. Hence it follows that this was the exact minute when Paul Simpson, in the cellar, within eight feet of the voice, and free from the deafness, heard only a sound, while they who stood by him understood the words plainly. The reality of the token appears from the undoubted veracity of Sally Wentworth, her inflexible opposition, and the oath of George Butler, the reputed dupe of the whole business.

[21] *Note from the original text:* She had come several times before, as the preceding letters show. Five months before this, Abner Blaisdell's son Paul and his sisters were sent by the ghost to a house where several young people were met for amusement; not for this purpose, but for terminating a difference between them and one of that company. The ghost strictly charged them to go and return in peace, and to abstain from all appearance of evil. The propriety of this small errand appears by its connections and the events which followed. But, as it stands insulated before the eyes of pride and folly, how despicable it must appear! Had such eyes looked on, when the first silk worm was formed, it would have appeared a trivial and useless contrivance. "As the heavens are higher than the earth; so are my ways higher than your ways, saith the Lord, and my thoughts than your thoughts." It would be very strange indeed, if a messenger from heaven should have much to perform in such a world as this, and yet meet with no opposition; and equally strange, if that messenger should perform nothing but what mankind would naturally expect, especially in a period when Christians themselves have not escaped the contagion of infidelity. *Editor's* Note: The fearful individual in Abner's family is none other than Lydia Blaisdell.

[22] *Note from the original text:* The children, through fear, had moved

their beds into the room where their parents lodged.

[23] The original edition incorrectly listed this date as August 11, 1800. See Note 5 above.

[24] Sentence in the original edition reads "his wife" instead of Lydia Blaisdell; to avoid confusion with the apparition of George Butler's former wife, the present edition uses the full name, Lydia Blaisdell.

[25] The original account incorrectly indicated that this took place on August 12th when it actually occurred the following evening. See Testimony of Joanna Hooper and Testimony of Capt. Paul Simpson.

[26] The initials probably signify "Paul Simpson, Sea Captain."

[27] This was Paul Blaisdell, who was spending the night at the house of James Miller in order to avoid another encounter with the specter. See Testimony of Paul Blaisdell.

[28] *Note from the original text:* These words were heard by eight persons.

[29] *Note from the original text:* This answer she now denies, but owns she saw the apparition.

[30] See also Deposition of Paul Simpson.

[31] Isaiah 40:3.

[32] *Note from the original text*: These enigmatical warnings were some of the first words which the voice uttered, and they appeared strange to us all. They appeared to be void of instruction, impertinent and utterly inapplicable to anything which was seen, remembered, or expected among us. None were then trifling with her; all wondered, and many were solemnized. Nor was there any remarkable contention among us. But after she had produced her strange, unexpected, unheard of message, our behavior soon fixed the meaning of these enigmas, and rendered them like apples of gold and pictures of silver. Her speaking so much in a by-place (a cellar) separate from the common dwelling of man, like John in the wilderness, has offended us. If her paths were the Lord's, instead of making them strait, we have made them crooked by misconception, misrepresentation, and falsehood. While the ghost was then speaking, one of the company was near eternity. Therefore "seek the Lord while he may be found." With what contempt and ridicule has the ghost been treated on account of the marriage! Therefore, "I am not to be trifled with" was pertinent. What violent contentions, occasioned by her messages, appropriate the terms "Peace, peace," or "there must be peace," as she more plainly said to another person about the same time.

[33] *Note from the original text:* Here we see that the direct answer was entirely avoided. It was no design of her mission. We have the Bible by which even the angels must be tried—to the law and the testimony. If they speak not according to this word, it is because they have no light in them, from whatever world they may profess to come.

She accordingly took this ground, and reasoned with the people out of the Scriptures as the standard of truth by which she would be tried.

[34] *Note from the original text:* It was a matter of trial to some Christians among us, that the Spirit should thus associate with one who never gave the least evidence of piety. But the Spirit informed them, out of her hearing, that Lydia Blaisdell was one of the elect, and would repent before she left the world.

[35] *Note from the original text:* "Don't you believe a word of all that I have told you," say some who heard it. She had several times fainted before.

[36] *Note from the original text:* A part of this testimony is lost.

[37] *Note from the original text:* She now talked without appearing. It was the next night after this, that the attempt was made to handle her while she appeared.

[38] *Note from the original text:* This shows that this witness was not in the cellar, when the preceding sentence was uttered. They who were there say that it was the Specter who said, *they must come down,* and Abner Blaisdell who added that *they should be satisfied.* Others tell us that the sentence was, "Come down *in order,* and you shall be satisfied." Make the worst of it; it was but innocent inaccuracy, like what is recorded of angels in the scriptures. Possibly the ghost did not foresee this confusion. Certain it is, that she constantly and strictly insisted upon order and solemnity, as indispensably requisite to her manifestations. After all, if the ghost has ever uttered one falsehood, or *one* false accusation, with the manifest design of injurious deception—or, if she has ever committed or ordered the commission of *one* crime—we must, without hesitation, condemn her as an evil angel. But then we must remember that her criminality should first be proved, not by our surmises or conjectures, but by substantial, plenary, and indubitable evidence.

[39] *Note from the original text:* Here is a little mistake. It was not her mother, but Abner Blaisdell who proposed this question, by her mother's desire expressed to him.

[40] The moon had been full the night before as reported in *Weatherwise's New Astronomical Diary; or an Almanack...Adapted to Maine* for August 1800.

[41] See also Deposition by Sarah Simpson.

[42] *Note from the original text:* This sentence was uttered at another time. It is believed by some, among whom is the writer, that several interviews mentioned in the last letter were not those of Nelly Hooper, but of another Specter. This may be somewhat difficult, and doubtless not essentially necessary, to prove.

[43] *Note from the original text:* That is, that they experienced the same.

[44] The original edition incorrectly listed this date as August 11. Accordingly, Paul Blaisdell's account of this encounter has been

moved to its present position to preserve his chronological order. See note 5 above.

[45] *Note from the original text:* "Before she vanished." That is, before she vanished for the last time that morning, for this was after she had vanished in the view of Richard Downing.

[46] The messengers were Lydia Blaisdell and her father Abner.

[47] *Note from the original text:* These last words declared to me by other witnesses are not in the original testimony of Joanna Hooper I have therefore enclosed them. Did Joanna Hooper assist in the work of personating her own daughter? If not, how could the deceiver know what questions she would ask? Do some of these things appear small? *Maxima minimis gaudent* (The greatest things are from among the least).

[48] *Note from the original text:* Her messages were probably such as never were since Christ was on earth. Some of them are contrary to all expectation, and exposed the families of Abner Blaisdell, David Hooper, George Butler, and Lydia Blaisdell, in particular, to unjust reproach. Therefore the loving kindness of the Lord to these families made the proofs as extraordinary as the messages, that whoever shall calumniate either of those families, on account of these events, may do it at their peril.

[49] *Note from the original text:* Richard Downing has since declared that he had found all these words to be true.

[50] *Note from the original text*: They saw no personal form.

[51] The original edition incorrectly listed this date as August 11, 1800. See note 5 above.

[52] *Note from the original text:* The order was nearly elliptical, for the two ranks were joined by certain persons at each end.

## Notes for Two 19ᵀᴴ Century Retellings

[1] Thomas Foss is in error here. He mistakes Lydia Blaisdell, born in 1785, with another Lydia Blaisdell, who was born in 1809. Clearly, Abner Blaisdell's fifteen-year-old daughter was not a spinster.

[2] This woman is not to be confused with Mary Gordon, whose testimony appears in this volume. Mary Gordon did not live nearby; she traveled a distance to witness the spirit at the Blaisdell House.

[3] Ambrose Simpson is in error here. Like Foss, Simpson mistakes the Lydia Blaisdell born in 1785 with the Lydia Blaisdell born in 1809. This latter woman's sister bore an illegitimate son, William H. Wooster. He was born in 1841 but he did not die in infancy.

## Notes for Genealogical Materials

[1] Genealogies prepared by Lois Crabtree Johnson are based on the following sources: Transcription of the Hooper Bible by Emery DeBeck; US Federal Census Reports for 1790-1860; 1798 Cobb Census

from Sullivan-Franklin, Maine; Vital records from Berwick, South Berwick, Franklin, Sullivan, York; Blaisdell Materials at the Sullivan-Sorrento Historical Society; Butler Materials at the Franklin Historical Society; Springer Materials at the Franklin Historical Society; Hooper Materials at the Franklin Historical Society.

## Notes for GEORGE BUTLER'S LAST WORD

[1] In addition to the documents included in the present edition, sources on the burning boat include the following: telephone interview with Emery DeBeck, local historian and genealogist who transcribed the Hooper Bible, 2 April 2008; Johnson, Lois Crabtree. 2001. "Genealogy, Gospel and Gossip." Hancock County Genealogical Society. 15 September. 1-5.

# RETELLINGS OF THE NELLY BUTLER HAUNTINGS:
## A PARTIAL LIST

## PRIMARY SOURCES

Cummings, Abraham. 1826. *Immortality Proved by the Testimony of Sense: in Which Is Contemplated the Doctrine of Spectres, and the Existence of a Particular Spectre. Addressed to the Candor of This Enlightened Age.* Bath, ME: Printed by J.G. Torrey.

Cummings, Abraham. 1859. *Immortality Proved by the Testimony of Sense: in Which Is Contemplated the Doctrine of Spectres, and the Existence of a Particular Spectre. Addressed to the Candor of This Enlightened Age.* Portland, ME: J.L. Lovell.

## RETELLINGS: A PARTIAL LIST

Almeder, Robert F. 1992. *Death and Personal Survival: The Evidence for Life after Death.* Boston: Rowman and Littlefield. 100-106, 121-131.

Anderson, Rodger I. 1983. "The Cummings Apparition." *The Journal of Religion and Psychical Research.* 6.3: 206-219.

--. "Blaisdell Family." 2006. *Psychics, Sensitives, and Somnambules: A Biographical Dictionary.* Jefferson: McFarland. 18-19.

Becker, Carl. 1993. *Paranormal Experience and the Survival of Death.* Albany: State University of New York Press. 194.

Bernard, Christine. 1977. "The Late Nelly Butler." *A Host of Ghosts.* New York: Lippincott. 27-35.

Bessor, John P. 1953. "The Return of Nelly Butler." *Fate Magazine.* 6.12 December. 36-41.

Blackwood, Gary L. 2000. *Spooky Spectres: Secrets of the Unexplained.* Tarrytown: Benchmark Books. 58.

Britten, Emma Hardinge. 1872. "Modern Spiritualism in America Prior to the Date of the Rochester Knockings." *The Western Star.*

July. 12-31.

--. 1884. "Wonderful Spiritual Manifestations in Maine in the Years 1800-1806." In *Nineteenth Century Miracles: Or, Spirits and their Work in Every Country of the Earth: A Complete Historical Compendium of the Great Movement Known as "Modern Spiritualism."* New York: W. Britten. 487-495.

Cahill, Robert Ellis. 1983. "America's First Ghost." *New England's Ghostly Haunts.* Peabody: Chandler-Smith. 6-8.

Citro, Joseph A. 1996. "The Machiasport Madonna." *Passing Strange: True Tales of New England Hauntings and Horrors.* Boston: Houghton. 33-38.

--. 2005. "A Mere Mass of Light." *Weird New England: Your Travel Guide to New England's Local Legends and Best Kept Secrets.* New York: Sterling. 184-185.

Dommeyer, Frederick. 1963. "Body, Mind, and Death." *Pacific Forum.*

Ducasse, C.J. 1961. *A Critical Examination of the Belief in a Life after Death.* Springfield: Charles Thomas. 21-23, 154-156.

Foss, Thomas. 1870. *A Brief Account of the Early Settlements along the Shores of the Skillings River, including West Sullivan, West Gouldsborough, Trenton Point and North Hancock.* Ellsworth: Sawyer. 14-16.

Grasso, Michael. 2004. *Experiencing the New World Now.* New York: Paraview. 53-55.

Haining, Peter. 1999. "Machias Ghost." *A Dictionary of Ghosts.* 1982. London: Robert Hale. 156.

Hauck, Dennis William. 2002. "Machiasport." *Haunted Places: The National Directory: Ghostly Abodes, Sacred Sites, UFO Landings, and Other Supernatural Locations.* 1994. New York: Penguin. 201.

LiBrizzi, Marcus. 2007. "America's Most Famous Ghost." *Dark Woods, Chill Waters: Ghost Tales from Down East Maine.* Camden:

Down East Books. 141-146.

Lund, David. 2009. *Persons, Souls, and Death: A Philosophical Exploration of an Afterlife.* Jefferson: Macfarland. 137-138.

McAdams, Elizabeth and Raymond Bayless. 1981. from "Ghosts and Witnesses." *The Case for Life after Death: Parapsychologists Look at the Evidence.* Chicago: Nelson-Hall. 41-43.

Norris, Curt. 1994. "America's First Ghost." *Yankee Magazine.* February. 58.2. 62.

O'Neil, J.P. 2003. *The Great New England Sea Serpent: An Account of Unknown Creatures Sighted by Many Respectable Persons between 1638 and the Present Day.* New York: Paraview. 19-23.

Pitkin, David J. 2002. "Nellie." *Ghosts of the Northeast.* Salem: Aurora. 298-299.

Roll, M. 1969. "A Nineteenth-Century Matchmaking Apparition: Comments on Abraham Cummings' *Immortality Proved by the Testimony of Sense." Journal of the American Society for Psychical Research.* 63, 396-409.

Sagendorph, Robb Hansell ed. 1957. "The Famous Specter of Bath, Maine." *The Old Farmer's Almanac Sampler.* New York: Washburn. 267-269.

Selzer, Adam. 2009. *Your Neighborhood Gives Me the Creeps: True Tales of an Accidental Ghost Hunter.* Woodbury: Llewellyn. 102-103.

Simpson, Ambrose. 1891. *Some Incidents of a Remarkable Reference Case Connected to Some of the Incidents of the Blaisdell Spirit that Created a Great Sensation about the Town of Sullivan, County of Hancock, about the Year 1800.* Bar Harbor: Record Job. 16-19.

Smith, Susy. 1971. *Confessions of a Psychic.* New York: Macmillan. 286-291.

--. 1967. "The Late Mrs. Nelly Butler." *Prominent American Ghosts.* Cleveland: World Publishing. 1-12.

Smith, Warren. 1968. "The Ghost Who Haunted a Town." *Strange Powers of the Mind.* New York: Ace. 132-137.

Sterling, Marvin C. 1993. *Philosophy of Religion: A Universalist Perspective.* Lanham: University Press of America. 156-157.

Stevens, C.J. 2002. "Encounters at Home." *The Supernatural Side of Maine.* Phillips: John Wade. 184-186.

Stevens, William Oliver. 1949. "Immortality Proved by the Testimony of Sense." *Unbidden Guests: A Book of Real Ghosts.* New York: Dodd, Mead, and Company. 261-269.

--. 1953. *Psychics and Common Sense: An Introduction to the Study of Psychic Phenomena.* New York: Dutton. 64-65.

Swann, Ingo. 1975. *To Kiss Earth Good-Bye.* New York: Hawthorne Books. 82.

Warner, John F. and Margaret B. Warner. 1987. "The Return of Nelly Butler." *Apparitions: 21 Stories of Ghosts, Spirits, and Mysterious Manifestations—with Exercises for Developing Critical Reading Skills.* Providence: Jamestown. 106-111.

Winehill, Pricilla. 1956. "It Takes a Certain Spirit to Bring out a Ghost." *The Blaisdell Papers.* 5.2 November. 45-47. Repeated in 1989 in 11.7. Winehill reprints the Sagendorph article with commentary.

Zwicker, Roxie J. 2007. "The Blaisdell House." *In Haunted Portland: From Pirates to Ghost Brides.* Charleston: Haunted America. 64-65.

Made in the USA
Las Vegas, NV
19 September 2021